THE AWAKENING OF RED FEATHER

JONATHON RAY SPINNEY

3rd Printing – October 1997

ISBN# 0-9651546-0-2

Medicine Bear Publishing
P.O. Box 1075
Blue Hill, ME 04614

This book is dedicated to all people who find the courage and strength to follow their dreams...and to the future return of dignity and honor to Native American spiritual philosophy.

50% of profits from this book will go towards material, spiritual, educational and legal needs of Native Americans.

PREFACE

THE AWAKENING OF RED FEATHER is based on profound personal experiences in which I became aware of the guiding presence of Christ and Native American spiritual healers on the continent of North America during these troubled times. The spirits of these beings are here among us helping to direct many people towards higher realms of understanding and light. This is the story of how, in one man's life, prophesy has been fulfilled and understood. Through dream, revelation, struggle and commitment, I have come to understand the prophesies of different cultures as expressions of the same truth about the ultimate purpose of human experience here on Earth. Today, many Native Americans wait patiently for the manifestation of a being they call the "Great White Brother" and "The Great Peacemaker". They wait for the great purification of Mother Earth and the return of real freedom and dignity for all people. Christians wait for the return of Christ and the trumpets of Revelation. They wait for the promised 1,000 years of peace and spiritual prosperity.

We are living in dangerous times. Mankind has made drastic mistakes in managing all aspects of our responsibility for life here on Earth. Our spiritual survival is now at stake because little or no respect for the land, the animals and the cultures native to all parts of this Earth has left the collective human soul empty and corrupt. With the coming of Christ, we shall see the restoration of that spiritual beauty of Native Americans with all the honor and dignity their philosophies deserve. He will come back with Sitting Bull, Chief Joseph and other great Native American leaders. All of the prominent spiritual leaders of humanity's past will incarnate in these end times to guide those willing to face truth and embrace love. This is the story of how I came to receive this information and how it has changed my life forever. We are now living during a climactic shift in the direction of human consciousness and spiritual awareness. Destruction in the material realm comes hand in hand with rebirth in the spiritual realm. Many cultures have prophesied the current global crisis and we are now living the prophesies. Humanity has re-emerged more than once in the past from global upheaval and destruction brought on by the disharmony and mistakes of political, dominant cultures. Evidence exists all over the world and in every scientific study of the Earth's past and humanity's past that there existed human cultures that were far more advanced in many ways beyond the current *modern* age. There is no doubt that we are heading for a new era of cultural destruction and re-birth. Humanity has been experiencing this for decades already. The Christian *Tribulation* is not a future event. We have been living the tribulation. The *Great Purification* prophecy of many Native cultures is not a future event. We are living the purification. *The Book of the Seven Seals* that is spoken of by St. John in Revelations is about to be opened. The truth of prophecy must be fulfilled.

There have been times, in recent months, that I have considered not writing this book for fear that it would not be of any value or importance to anyone but myself. But I believe there are many other people around the world experiencing a higher force at work in their lives and are being awakened to more profound spiritual consciousness. I have realized how important it is to share with others our spiritual growth as much as possible. I am not a prophet. I am not a spiritual master. My life has been difficult and full of mystical experience. I have worked hard to educate myself in order to be able to share the knowledge I have gained about humanity's past and future with others. I no longer question the spiritual experiences of my life or why they occur... I just go on in faith that the Creator will reveal to me someday the ultimate purpose of my being. Through these words, I offer other people only a grain of truth to the vast beach of human spiritual understanding. This is all that I can do and I pray that it will be of some help to even a few souls attempting to strengthen their faith and belief in Christ, Native American philosophy, and the reality of higher forces of love and purpose overshadowing the increasing turmoil and struggle of human experience...

To those who doubt the reality of Christ and the prophesies of his return and to those who have experienced the many perilous deceptions and evils cast about in this world by many religions in the name of *Christ* (and there have been a multitude), I can only relate what I have learned through deep, transforming personal experience. Human beings must believe in the powers of the Divine, for we are living in a world that is out of control and heading for terrible social disaster. Somewhere in the whole drama of *Western* human experience our Creator had to emerge as an individual to direct us toward universal love and forgiveness because these ways of being are our only hope for survival. Our Creator has emerged in many other cultures through great leaders but, unfortunately the institutions of Christianity have tried to eclipse these truths, leaving many people around this world lost and angry; eager to reject Christ or any great leader, male or female, who exemplified the message of universal love. Our Creator emerges in every one of us every day to fulfill the destiny of humanity. This is the story of our Creator's emergence in me and in my life through emotional and physical trauma, personal sacrifice, and eventual spiritual understanding.

CHAPTER I

THIS MORNING THE SCARLET DAWN penetrated my consciousness and caused me to remember; it was exactly nine years ago today that I had the dream. How unaware I was of my purpose in life, living day-to-day, following the shadows of my emotional self and trying to heal from childhood pain and abandonment. And now, looking down into those soft, icy fields across the way, I feel the chill of that awakening to the truth of prophecy and the awesome realization of the Creator's hand at work today on this planet. I was twenty-eight then and that dream stirred my unconscious mind like a great meteor plunging into an eternally still lake, forever changing the face of that reality. Since the dream and the seven year drama that unfolded after it, I stand in awe of the archangels and the higher forces of good. I have given my heart and soul to their will and have become only an instrument in their desperate attempt to restore the original idea of love and beauty for humanity as they fight those growing forces of darkness. I have no doubts about the power of eternal love and the promise of Christ's return and the return of Native American spiritual dignity. Please, let me tell you this story. It comes from truth and from one person's attempt to grasp the deeper realities of his existence and his relationship to the whole of humanity as one Soul... one Light.

It seems that we spend most of our lives as human beings attempting to find meaning and purpose - anything to grab hold of that we can believe and know is real. The material world comes and goes. Things change and end as new experiences begin. One thing that never changes, though, is the evolving essence of what and who we are. Before the dream, I had experienced many spiritual awakenings but was still adrift in the vast ocean of souls, living my life with little solid faith and commitment. I was a carpenter-builder and occasionally expressed myself creatively through music and painting. I lived in a log cabin that I hand-built and had no bills to speak of, and no great pressures from society nor obligations to anyone. I spent a lot of time in the forest as it was a healing time for me and a time for natural experience. Little did I know all of that was about to change forever.

I awoke one cold January night from a dream, shaking uncontrollably and completely energized by some great impulse of energy. My body felt strange for days after while I tried to understand what I had seen. The first thing that I saw happen in the dream was a brilliant explosion of orange and yellow light which flashed across my life, my home, and my inner being. I could see myself out in the cabin yard cutting and shaping a huge pine log, with wood chips and sawdust flying everywhere. I was watching myself creating a totem pole with a great eagle on the top. The eagle had a wide wing span and was partially in flight. I remember faces, symbols and colors but one thing caught my attention more than any other part of the dream: it was the face of a great Chief or Native Shaman staring out of the totem pole directly into my soul.

As I worked on through the night in the dream, I was aware that some mystical force was acting through the *me* that was carving this sculpture. The eagle was incredible. Its wings were at least 10 or 12 feet across and its face was strong and perfect. I remember painting brilliant reds, blues, sunburst yellow and turquoise. I painted in detail symbols that made no sense to me at the time and for many years afterward. Just before I awoke, though, is when the face of the Chief came alive. With a look that pierced my heart and soul, he began to speak: "I am Red Feather, Jonathon. I have come back to find my people and fulfill our prophecy. I will guide you to create what you see before you. We will take the totem on a long journey to the West, as it must be done." The Chief then emerged from the log and rose before me as I was now in my body and was directly experiencing the dream rather than viewing it from above. He said a prayer while he waved a large eagle feather over my heart:

Shaa nee ah te lena
Shaa nee ah te naya
Shaa nee ah te lena
Shaa nee ah te naya

Then he seemed to float above and around me while he gradually transformed into an eagle. I saw one red feather on the breast of the eagle as it entered into my body to some deep reality within. I was awake now shaking, tired and totally confused about what had happened in the dream.

The days following were intense and full of apprehension. I had never even seen a totem pole and had never carved anything bigger than a 10-inch owl, let alone a 12-foot eagle. The totem in the dream was 20 feet long or more and was massive. How could I create such a thing? Weeks passed and I got busy with other creative activities and in time forgot the dream. I married and moved farther out into the country. Eventually we had two sons. There were large pine trees on the property as well as beautiful fields and streams. Things were fine for a year or so. Then I awoke one night to see the eagle Red Feather looking at me through the window with tears of hurt and sadness as if totally abandoned. I got out of bed feeling an overwhelming pain in my heart.

I guess I made the commitment that night to Red

Feather, to the Creator, and to myself that I was going to create that totem. For the next three or four years I worked every spare moment on totem poles and eagles. I was so intense that every thought revolved around my sculptures. During that time, my life changed dramatically as my inner self was being transformed through the process of creating and the commitment. My spirituality was developing during this time and the boys' mother and I eventually grew apart. She was not ready for the responsibilities of a family and, perhaps, I was not ready for the responsibilities of a relationship. She finally left to find her own path and the boys and I did our best to hold our family together.

I chiseled, carved, sanded and painted day after day, trying to create the totem of the dream. I must have carved 20 totems with 20 eagles before I could figure out how to do the wings in flight. There were times when my hands and fingers throbbed from pain and overwork, because I also worked at my trade to support my sons and keep up my life. Every extra cent I had went into tools, paints and increasingly larger logs.

Finally, after years of work and preparation, I had a huge 25-foot pine log delivered to the carving yard. I knew it was the one, but the massive size of it confounded me. How was I going to move it around... let alone transport it to the West? The first totems were heavy, but I could stand them up with the help of five or six people. This log defied all attempts by human muscle to even budge it. Frustrated, I let two or three months go by before I could bring myself around to start work on this giant pine. But after a while, I started working on the eagle, shaping, sanding, and fitting the wings until I was satisfied that it was all exactly as it had been in the dream. I remember the day I painted the red feather on the glossy black breast of the eagle: I felt relieved and from then on the rest of the creation went well. It took me a year to finish the totem. I wanted to carve every detail that I had seen in the dream and paint it with the exact colors. I developed a process of resin coated, waterproofed paints which proved to be strong and durable. For the Chief's face I used a piece of cedar, implanted into the pine log, as cedar looked more like natural skin. When it was finally finished, I went to work buying a trailer and building a cradle in which to set the totem so that I could safely transport it across the country. I had to hire heavy equipment to help move it around, but I learned how to deal with its massive size.

Six years had passed now, and I wondered if it was time to leave with the totem. I had been having dreams over those years and I knew that the totem was to go to the Hopi Nation in Arizona. At that time, I knew very little about the Hopi people and did not even know where in Arizona their homeland was. But I had faith that I would come to know these things when the time was right. My problem for that moment was to figure out how I could come up with enough money and courage to uproot my sons and second wife, Jessie, from our home in the wooded hills of Maine. I wondered what I was getting us all into.

As I saved and worked to prepare for the journey, an increasing urgency developed in my soul about leaving. I kept putting the date up closer and working harder to get things ready, for there was a lot to be done. I outfitted the pickup, designed a travel seat for my sons and installed a camper top. Hundreds of dollars were needed but somehow it all came together. The hardest part of it all, though, was leaving our home. We all loved it there and our lives were simple but full. We always had had a great garden, plenty of wild berries and good hunting and fishing. I knew that we had to go but we would miss our home and friends. That home was the only peace and security I had even known and now I was leaving it heading into the unknown. I was not even sure where I was headed, but I hung on to my vision and prayed that everything would be all right. It was October 1st, 1990, and we were on the road.

It did not take long for me to realize that the pickup and trailer were critically overloaded. I had put extra log pieces on the back of the trailer for future carvings because I had become really interested in the craft. We had to stop and throw off some of the weight and rearrange things. Everything we owned was with us, for I had closed up the house completely, not knowing when we would ever be back. Those first nights on the road were scary for all of us. My sons were losing contact with their mother. Jessie was hoping this journey would bring us closer together because our relationship had not been good as it had been based on the needs of the boys rather than our own. I was hoping to get us out in the vicinity of Arizona safely and find us a place to live. I think we all cried a little as we headed into the unknown. The weather, as we traveled out of New England, was bad and it rained all the way to Ohio. I had real doubts about my sanity and tried to justify constantly within myself what I was doing. Had I lost my mind? Was I being selfish by expecting my family to follow me while I was following a mystical dream? The trailer was incredibly heavy and I had to be fully alert all the time. It was not easy to pull a giant totem pole with a 12-foot eagle through the jammed highway interchanges in St. Louis and other big cities. Actually, it was very dangerous. But we kept moving West and made better time than I had expected.

By the time we hit the Texas Panhandle, I was exhausted mentally, emotionally and physically. It had all hit me somewhere in Missouri: what had I done? Where was I going and what did it all mean? We made plans to go first to El Paso and spend a few days with my grandmother because I had not seen her for many years. The trip had put us all on edge by now and my sons, five and six years old, were going stir crazy confined to the back of the pickup. I turned south in Texas toward southern New Mexico looking for the direct route to El Paso. It was a good feeling to hit New Mexico for reasons we found out later. I had not really paid close attention to the maps, though, and the major highway route I had chosen turned out to be heading right through a mountain chain and through the Apache Indian Territory. There was a stiff west wind that day and the truck did okay until we had climbed to 8,000 feet. From then on we barely made 10 miles per hour and the engine was very hot. I had never experienced panic such as the panic I felt that afternoon when we climbed up over those passes.

The fear I had was for my family. What if the engine blew? What would I have done? I desperately tried to calm myself. I put the truck into its lowest gear and after two or three hours we reached the summit. There we saw the sun in the western sky, gloriously shining on the most beautiful forest I had ever seen. We were on Apache land now, going downhill toward White Sands. That afternoon, on Apache land, was where I felt the power of all that was happening in my life. Much of my fear, anxiety and worry turned to courage, hope and peace. We had made it over those mountains against a very hot, persistent wind. I had overcome all obstacles thus far. For more than six years I had struggled: how could I give up now?

Late that night we drove into El Paso. We were very happy to find my grandmother's house. She had beds ready for us – our first and foremost need. That night I dreamed again. It was the first time in a while that I had received some immediate direction: I was not to go into Arizona yet, rather I was to go north into the Sangre de Cristo Mountains. At the time, I did not know that the English translation is the "Blood of Christ" mountains. I would find out later that it was no accident for us to be there in those mountains for the winter. For that night, though, we needed rest and for the next three days we relaxed and got to know my grandmother. When I awoke the first morning there, I immediately went out to check the trailer for it held the totem and all of our belongings.

While I was tightening ropes I happened to look up toward the east at the Franklin Mountains. A crimson glow on the hillside revealed the image of a great thunderbird. I was shocked at first as it seemed very much like my totem eagle. I felt a wave of spiritual energy rush through me and was excited about the future. I knew that, in time, some revelation would unfold from this strange journey. I had found out later that the Natives had always considered the mineral outcropping on the mountain to be very sacred. They believed the thunderbird protected the north-to-south continental passage along the Rio Grande. I felt protection that morning, and in a few days we were heading north.

Southern New Mexico is vast. Desert plains stretch for miles to meet jagged volcanic mountains. We drove farther north each hour and by mid-afternoon we reached Santa Fe and the foothills of the Sangre de Cristos. We all were astounded by the magical beauty of northern New Mexico. The trip from Santa Fe to Taos late that afternoon was one I'll never forget. The only pass to Taos heading north from Santa Fe is along the Rio Grande River. It was sunset by then and the cliffs and canyon walls along the river were radiating spectrums of red and brown. Giant cottonwood trees lined the river in places, interrupted occasionally by small orchards and vegetable gardens. It was harvest time along the Rio Grande and we took the time to share in the blessings of another season passing. I felt that the gorge entrance to the Taos plains and the heart of the Cristo Mountains, was like a gate. We had come a long way and I was now entering a different experience of consciousness and reality. Letting go of fears was a big issue for me. Even my sons had grown in a special way. Our love had deepened, and their trust in me increased my trust in the purpose of why I was there, even though I did not understand where it all would lead.

For the next week we stayed here and there around the Taos area. I went through a period of panic about finding a home for my family and a place to set up a studio. Rents were high in Taos, but my trust in the purpose of my being there held us all together. The periods of panic dissolved away into the breathtaking panoramas of the Taos plains, the Taos and the Sangre de Cristos. We all felt a sense of honor and good fortune for being able to experience the beauty of it all. The totem and other sculptures on the trailer were attracting interest everywhere we went, but we needed a home for the winter and I needed space to prepare myself for the next part of the journey. At the end of our first week in and around the Cristo Mountains we found an old adobe and wood house deep in the mountain valley of Amalia. The rent was cheap and the natural beauty of the valley was beyond words. Wild herds of elk and deer became a common sight for us. We were surrounded by high forested peaks and rock cliffs of quartz and mineral rich soil. Soon the snow came and the pangs of day to day survival took over.

CHAPTER II

L ATE OCTOBER IN AMALIA was beautiful. The days were warm and the nights were cold but fresh and alive. We were at 8,500 feet up in the Rio Costilla Valley, surrounded by mountain peaks rising up to 12,000 feet and higher. By now the cottonwood leaves were returning quickly to the pastures and rivers banks of the valley floor, exposing the reality of nature and things to come. The small adobe-wood home we rented was only a stone's throw away from the river and at night we could hear the clear water whisper past the house like a healing song. We had settled in comfortably and I had put up two or three cords of firewood. The days were getting shorter and the snows came early. I felt as though my mind was flooded with some strange energy. We all felt it and were changing by the day. There is something special about those mountains. Only the Creator or God could understand... or perhaps the Native people who still live there *in spirit*.

"When winter comes so does the dream time." I remembered that from one of the books I had read before the trip out. My interest in Native American philosophy had developed strongly during the five or six years working on the totems. That winter in Amalia brought us all the experience of dreamtime as my sons, Jessie, and I all started having strong, vivid dreams every night. Jonathon, my younger son, had started waking up in trance-like states that resembled the trances that Native Shamans would enter during their ceremonies. He could see another reality and would tell me to "look". Every time he went into one of these trance-like states, he would say, "Dad, do you see it... look Dad... hurry!" I grew very concerned for he was very tired and weak after those experiences. They began coming more frequently and even in his conscious hours. One afternoon, he was playing in the snow with his brother Jason when he almost lost consciousness and fell down. Jason managed to get him up and into the house as Jonathon was again in another trance-like state. At this point, I decided to seek medical advice for there was a swelling near his left eye after that afternoon trance.

Later that night on the way to the hospital, I was feeling that something was not right in Amalia. Within the vast and overwhelming beauty, there seemed to be something to fear. I had learned, since our arrival there, that Amalia was an old Spanish ranching valley and that the history of the families there was marred by greed and hate. The Spanish had come into the valley hundreds of years before and had claimed the land from the Native Peoples. *In the name of Christ*, the Spanish prospered in the valley for it was rich with wildlife, minerals, forests, and fish. There were natural pastures along the river for many miles and ranching thrived, bringing wealth to all the Spanish families in the valley. Out on the plains though, where the Rio Costilla headed out of the valley towards the Rio Grande, the less successful Spanish families had settled and planted beans. During years of low water, the families in the valley would control the water to keep their pastures rich and green, while the bean farmers would lose many of their crops. There had been fighting, stealing and even murder in the shadows of the Sangre de Cristos. I thought of these things during the two-hour ride into Pueblo, Colorado, and I realized that there was some *negative* or evil energy present in that valley. But my concern for the moment was Jonathon and the altered states of consciousness he was experiencing.

I had been directed to Pueblo by doctors in Taos because there were no other cities around that could offer the medical specialists that Jonathon needed. We spent hours in Pueblo that night and then returned two or three times to talk with neurologists and other specialists. They had performed MRI brain scans, nerve tests, blood tests and complete physicals. Nothing could be found at all... he was perfectly healthy. I knew that something mysterious was going on but I felt no fear. Instead I felt as though we had all become human receivers to some other realm. I had seen big changes in all of us. Jessie was more spiritually aware now and recognized her need to heal emotionally. I was aware of the same need in myself. I started painting and carving and found that I had more profound ability to *channel* ideas onto canvas and into wood than I had ever experienced before. Still, I needed to provide for my family and, for the time being, the eagle totem laid covered with tarps like some sleeping statue waiting to come alive.

Around mid-December, a southern wind blew into the valley bringing two or three warm days. Much of the snow that had fallen thus far melted away into the Rio Costilla. The boys, Jessie, and I decided to hike up into a deep cliff lined canyon above our house. In early December, I, too, had started to have strange spells of altered consciousness which left me exhausted and confused for a few hours, but I was feeling great that day and anxious for a long hike. The canyon was an amazing place. Piles of splintered and chewed deer and elk bones lay under cliffs, cast down by ancient mountain lions. We got a glimpse of one lion for just an instant when it was awakened by our voices as we climbed up through the rocks and the twisted, washed-out cracks of the canyon floor. This was a sacred place... almost forbidden. I sensed the importance to leave things as we found them and not to disturb the area at all. We climbed on though, as I also felt the need to reach the uppermost end of the canyon that was guarded by huge spiral columns of stone. The canyon was ablaze with fire as the rays from the southwestern sun reached deep within the cliffs, illuminating for a few short moments places that were almost always in shadows and darkness.

There was a point during the climb where it became extremely difficult and dangerous to go on. Ice and snow covered the rocks and washouts. We came across a giant boulder sitting right in the path ahead, as if some force or some ancient people had left it there to block the final entrance to the canyon's heart. The boulder had no resemblance to the surrounding rocks and cliffs and it stood out dramatically from every other rock in the canyon. I was able to find a way around it though, and guided my family up into the next canyon level. They had become tired and were afraid to go much farther and I almost turned back. But I couldn't go back... not yet. I needed to experience that *forbidden* place as I had the feeling that I would be a different person after that day. For months I had been little by little letting go of my old self, creating a vast openness within me for new experience and change. It seemed that somehow this canyon was meant to fill that need. I found a warm alcove where Jessie and the boys could sit and asked them to wait for me. I would not be long for I could see the canyon's end just a short climb ahead. When I reached the place where the cliffs came together and became one with the mountain, I knew that I had reached a new beginning in my life. Many times before, I had had that feeling but never had I felt it so strong. A sense of overwhelming fate pervaded my soul as I prayed to the Creator for guidance and strength. The power of that mountain seemed to release itself at the canyon's end and

I offered my prayer of thanks immersed in nature's awesome force of solitude. I could not stay there long for the children were calling. They were getting cold and I needed to get them all home safely. We had climbed 1,500 feet up to 10,000 feet or so from the valley floor. We were all short of breath by then as we had not lived long in high altitude. We made good time on the trip down and soon were back in the warm comfort of the Amalia adobe. I filled the wood stove to the brim and that night the memory of the canyon still echoed in our souls.

I remember being worried later that evening as I watched Jessie paint a dry root-stick that she had picked up on the way out of the canyon. It had the head of an eagle already formed on it and also the image of a whale. This was interesting because we had found sea shells up at 10,000 feet. She decided to make a rattle with the root, and that night she asked one of the local Spanish ranchers with whom we had become friends if he had any rattles from mountain rattlesnakes. He had some and said he would drop them by the next day. With very little paint, the images of the eagle and the whale came fully to life. It was beautiful, but I was concerned and told Jessie it was not wise to acquire another person's *medicine* objects. I also told her not to evoke power from the animal spirits without the knowledge of how to use and direct it properly. I had learned from reading and from my experience with Native Americans not to fool around with such forces without the right spiritual foundation. But she was committed as if some power was acting through her. I went to sleep that night very apprehensive but trusted in my faith and the purpose of why we were all there.

The following morning, our friend brought over the dried rattles. I had decided not to say anything more to her about my concerns. I have always believed that fear itself is an energy that can bring into your life the very thing you fear. I asked the rancher if he knew anything about the canyon. He would not say much... only that nobody ever goes up there. He had been in Amalia most of his life and had been up there once as a child. After Jessie completed the rattle, she handed it to me. As I held it I knew that it could manifest a strong power, maybe even a dangerous power. I got a piece of moose hide and showed her how to wrap it up and keep it put away.

Around noontime that day, I became weak and very ill. Within two or three hours I could hardly hang on to my conscious state. My body was in total pain and I was overcome with fever. I asked Jessie to call the rancher who had brought her the rattles. He came over and I managed to arrange a ride to the hospital in Taos, fifty miles away. I wanted Jessie to stay with the boys and keep things stable for the moment because I was uncertain of what was unfolding. I knew I was very sick and wondered if I would survive whatever was attacking me. Never had I experienced such total pain and confusion. I could barely stay conscious during the ride to Taos. By the time we arrived at the hospital, I was in a paralyzed, semi-conscious state. I cannot remember anything more about that night or the hospital. I only remember going to a place far away from conscious reality and far away from my ego self.

Back in Amalia, Jessie received a call from the hospital requesting more information about me because I was unable to answer many questions. For two or three days I was in and out of consciousness and running a high fever. The doctors were taking every test that they could to determine how to treat me, but all the tests came back negative. Jessie was told to contact other family members as there were doubts about my pulling through those first days. I guess that even I thought it was the end at one point. I couldn't accept the thought of being paralyzed and asked God to please not leave me in that condition. After making arrangements for the boys' care, Jessie came down to see me that first morning. I was awake for a short while between unconsciousness, sleep and dreaming. I told her about a dream I had just awakened to... how she needed to hold the rattle and go around the house stopping at each direction to shake the rattle four times. She had opened us all up to a powerful force with her creation and now had to learn to use it to protect us. Whatever was happening to me had a direct relationship to that rattle. It bothered her immensely to hear my words, but she went back to Amalia and followed my instructions the following day. It was at that point that I started to get better. The strangest thing about my illness was the fact that my right arm had the appearance of a snake bite. The doctors felt sure that I had been bitten by something. In any case, I left the hospital five or six days later, still weak and sore, but recovering.

To this day, I cannot tell myself or anyone else exactly what happened to me after the canyon visit and the following illness. I do know that I was cared for in the hospital by a Native woman from the Taos Pueblo while, at the same time, Jessie had formed a relationship with a woman named Georgia in Amalia. Georgia was Native American and married to a Spanish-Anglo man. They were sort of outcasts in a valley of Spanish ranchers but were good people, as I came to know. They were always ready and willing to help those in need. I am able to look back now and see that there was a strong Native American spiritual force at work in my life during that time. Even the physical collapse I had endured was part of a purification process. As we got to know Georgia and her husband, we joined them occasionally when they attended a Mormon church in Colorado. I could not relate to the Mormon system of religion, but I was shocked to find out about the Book of Mormon which they studied along with the Bible. The Book of Mormon is the story of the *lost tribes* (Native Americans) and the appearance of Christ on this continent about 2,000 years ago. The book tells of his performing miracles and pro-phesying the coming of a greedy, destructive race of people to their lands which would lead to tremendous spiritual change on Earth.

Learning this was a major awakening for me, and I realized that I was being educated to some truth by a higher spiritual force. My whole time of consciousness in the hospital had been filled with one vision or dream after another. I had worried too, about the totem. I needed to fulfill the responsibility concerning the totem, but strange events and circumstances had taken over, forcing me to grow and strengthen quickly. It seemed that I had gained in spiritual understanding most of all, which is, as I have come to know, the only lasting reality of our existence. All else comes and goes, and the material comforts and wants of life, although necessary, can often block the development of our souls. To find the balance is, I think, the real challenge of being human.

CHAPTER III

T HE EVENTS OF AMALIA really were not all that strange, considering the many challenging and often spiritual experiences that had shaped my mind and soul throughout my life. Fear of change or fear of death were realms of being that never had a chance to grow within me. As a child, I had never known stability, for my mother divorced my father when I was two years old and moved my sister and me back and forth across the country for several years. She married again when I was five and, for a while, I had a stepfather who was a cold, selfish alcoholic. That marriage fell apart about the same time we lost our house to a San Diego mudslide in 1965. My mother developed a rare blood disease and became very ill physically and emotionally. The following years were difficult and full of great responsibility for me. I cooked, cleaned, did laundry and worked nights after school for extra money to buy bread and milk. My mother was receiving welfare but oftentimes spent it wastefully. She became progressively abusive, both mentally and physically and, when I was fifteen, the State of California became the guardian for me, my sister and two brothers. My sister and I were sent to a foster home on the outskirts of San Diego while plans were made for us to fly up to Maine to live with our biological father.

I think all children, with few exceptions, are born with a spirit of peace and innocence that remains whole until disrupted, repressed or destroyed by parents or society. I remember this one dream in particular that I had when I was a child. I would be experiencing a smooth flow of energy or soft waves inside of and around me that would suddenly become all scattered, painful and chaotic. I would feel warmth and security change to fear and anxiety. Those dreams began about the age of two; the same time I remember my parents arguing and fighting violently during the night. My whole life has been an effort to find or return to the original state of being that is natural to my soul. During the short stay at the foster home, I felt peace for the first time in over ten years and was able to heal a little from some of the emotional wounds.

I had been living at the foster home for one week when one day I was invited to go to the beach with a friend. It was stormy that day and the waves at La Jolla Beach were higher than normal. We were warned that riptide or undercurrents were strong, but the high waves were just too inviting for raft surfing. We were having the time of our lives when suddenly I felt it coming - a powerful undercurrent pulling at my feet. I felt the sand under me caving away. Desperately, I did exactly what you are not supposed to do; I tried to swim against it. It was only a matter of thirty seconds or so before the force of the ocean sucked me under for two or three hundred yards and out to sea. I felt panic and fear at first and saw my whole life pass by me in an instant. As my lungs filled with water, there was no pain and my panic turned to peace.

The force of the ocean, which at first terrified me, now was overwhelmingly beautiful. My soul seemed to merge with this force as I felt a great sense of vastness and wonder. My body was just tossed around in the tide, but the something that was me was suddenly above the whole scene. The feeling I had at this time escapes all description, but I remember the peace and beauty of it. It seemed that the normal sense of time had no meaning in this realm and I felt, for the first time, really free. Then the experience really deepened. Behind me, or above me, was a bright light. As I focused on the light, I saw the most beautiful person radiating love and light towards me. I had never had any religious upbringing and no one had ever exposed me as a child to the Bible nor Jesus. I did not really know at the time who this radiant being was but I knew he or she was reaching out to me. It seemed a million miles away, but the being was so perfect, so clear and full of light. Between the radiant being and me there were many jagged mountains and deep, dark valleys. I wanted to be with that being and go into the light, but suddenly I could see the ocean scene near the beach again. A lifeguard had spotted me when I first went under, and had come down to the beach in a rescue vehicle. He had swum out to my body, tied a float line on me, and was pulling me in. I can still remember being right above the scene, watching, in amazement, his strong strokes pulling my limp body towards the shore. Seconds later, I was coughing, spitting and choking on the sand, with a crowd of people around. I was sad. A great feeling of despair came over me. I got up and calmly thanked the lifeguard and told my friend that I needed to go back to the foster home. Two weeks later I was on my way to Maine to meet my father.

My life had been changed forever that day, but for years I blocked out the experience. It wasn't until the age of twenty that I began to dream about the drowning and had a deep feeling that I needed to get busy and do something with my life. Thus, I enrolled with the Outward Bound program at the University of Maine and studied theology and philosophy. Those nights when I read the New Testament were very special and sacred to me and I longed for that light to again pervade my soul. Slowly but surely, over many years, the drowning experience eventually became a powerful truth in my life.

The being that I had seen was Christ and I had felt his universal and unconditional love.

Somewhere along the way, I realized that the mountains and valleys that I had seen in my vision indicated the distance between the spiritual peace of Christ love and my inner self, and that my whole future life would be a journey over these mountains and valleys to merge with the truth of the light I had seen. I think that growing up with no spiritual foundation at all is worse than growing up with a false one, for at least you have something to believe in. On this vast sea of life and in the vast sea of human emotion, each soul must be able to know and hold onto something solid— some faith, ideal or belief system that leads to the understanding of universal love. Looking back, I can see that my life could have easily gone a self-destructive route had I not experienced those moments of death and the beyond. I thank God, the Creator and all the higher forces of good for that experience. I have developed a solid faith based on this experience but developing this faith did not come easily for I could not relate the experience of what I had seen to other people without being considered crazy or off the wall. So, for many years, I just blocked it out. This was where I was when I left the foster home for the journey to Maine.

You could say that my sister and I were excited about getting a fresh start in life with the parent we never knew. After a few days at my father's house that excitement turned to disappointment and pain. My father was a severe alcoholic in the advanced stages of self-abuse. Thank God for my stepmother! She held it all together the best she could but I collapsed into a period of depression and anxiety that lasted for a year or so. My sister handled it by getting pregnant and married at sixteen just to get away from the parental abuse. I left my father's house at seventeen and got two jobs working seven days a week to afford my own apartment. I went to night classes for my high school diploma. There was a tremendous level of hurt, unfounded guilt and emotional turmoil in my soul by the time I reached eighteen. The next two years were terrible for me and I would never want to relive them. They were terrible in the sense that I was lost... totally lost. The spiritual truths of the drowning experience had not yet dawned in my conscious mind.

At that time in my life there was a natural and native awareness attempting to develop within me. The friends I had met shortly after arriving in Maine were very abusive towards women, animals and the natural world in general. This bothered me and I did not fit in with them. I could not find pleasure in shooting wild squirrels or songbirds for Saturday afternoon fun. When I walked out in the forest, I felt peace and a deep sense of oneness. These feelings of oneness with nature became intense around the age of eighteen and I found myself wanting to be out in the woods every chance I could. It was also hard for me to come to grips with my father's ways and the attitudes of his family and friends. He lived in the small mill town of Old Town on the Penobscot River. Within Old Town, on an island in the river, there was and still is today the Penobscot Indian Reservation. In 1970, when I arrived in Maine, it was the Anglo mentality to exploit the Penobscots and to treat them with hypocritical prejudice. Even my father boasted with his friends about going on the reservation at night to sleep with tribal women. All of this made me sick as I became increasingly aware of the reality of society in that area. I could not let myself become a part of that destruction of human dignity, nor could I find it within myself to disrespect a woman of any race. I was different I guess, which made me a loner oftentimes, but I continued to strive for self-realization and the healing experience I found in nature.

It was the Maine woods, rivers, streams and sharp seasonal changes that brought me the first real experience of wholeness I had known in my life. I was still very lost emotionally and spiritually but I was committed to not becoming like my father. He had shown me all the things not to be and I see now the necessary purpose of my path with him. We cannot condemn the people in our past that may have caused us pain as they usually turn out to be the seeds of growth, change and self-realization in our own lives. I've had to learn to love and forgive to be able to find any peace within myself and, if any one of them be judged, it would not be my place, position or desire. Besides, I have come to understand that my father and I have been healers for each other. I see it as the magic of love underlying all chaos and pain!

During those years of emotional confusion and drifting, I let go of my parents. I remember the exact moment in time that this happened within my heart and soul. It was on the cliffs of Monterey back out on the Pacific coast. I had hitch-hiked across country to see my mother... hoping that she had gotten better but found her cold, angry and unstable. She blamed me for the intervention of Child Protection Services in her life four or five years earlier. I knew it was not my fault as I was only a child then, trying to hold it all together. I just couldn't go on watching my younger sister and brothers being beaten and emotionally abused. My visit this time was short as I knew there was no relationship at all to build on, and I had to put distance between us. For two or three days I traveled up the west coast until that afternoon at Monterey. That afternoon turned out to be a major turning point in my emotional growth. Lying on the cliffs overlooking the western seas, I was crying out, hurt and angry, asking; "If there be any God or loving Creator; why then did I have to be so hurt by my parents?" I can remember wanting to blame someone or some unknown force for my turmoil as the setting sun cast a gold glow over the cliffs and into my mind late that afternoon. I had lain there for hours watching the ocean resigned to my pain and anguish and shook at times while re-living my drowning in those waters years earlier. It was within the golden glow that I was somehow released from my pain and grief. I transcended the emotional anguish and I felt or heard within that I did have parents... good parents. I came to know the warm and brilliant sun as my father. Later that night, the rising full tinted moon became my mother. Somehow that realization brought me enough peace and security to really let go of the hurt and go on in my life. I knew then that there was nothing for me in California anymore. I left the Pacific coast that night for Maine determined to create a better life, free from the afflictions of my parents.

Even in those days, the difficulties and tribulations that I experienced were forming me and, perhaps, directing me to develop a more spiritual atonement to life. Life brings us all difficulties and no one can easily escape the need to grow spiritually through addictions or in the shadow masks of decaying social fortitude. There were periods all through my early twenties when I tried those escape routes but they never worked. I kept having re-occurring dreams about my drowning in the Pacific, which always left me longing to again experience the feeling of universal oneness. The vision of Jesus in the afterlife would flash in my mind, but I still could not grasp the larger meaning of the experience or relate personally to "Christ" or "God". This experience came later after my reading the New Testament in college. It was then that I was struck by the natural and simple beauty so pervasive within the core message of Jesus. I did not understand how Churches could make it so often confusing and complicated.

It has become clear to me over time that there were two distinct paths of spiritual understanding opening up to me during those years. I came to understand Christianity while studying theology and philosophy in college. This was mostly a mental experience; rational and historical and only personal during the times that I reflected on or dreamed about the afterlife. At the same time, I was learning to develop my sense of oneness with all life and thus I became very interested in the Native American spiritual beliefs. The latter understanding was almost always very mystical and would come to me in the most unexpected times. Sometimes I would have flashes of intuition about the connectedness of all things. Other times I would actually have a real mysterious and magical experience in the outer world. One of these experiences began when I was about half way through college and continued on and off for over five years.

While walking in an old pine forest near the University of Maine, I stumbled on some odd shaped mounds covered with leaves and rotting pine needles. My curiosity aroused, I started poking around the mounds and, to my amazement, found that they were hollow and had lids made of woven branches and bark strands. Inside, there were hundreds of upright branches all neatly woven together with cedar bark to form a round cylinder which extended into the ground a foot or two. In the bottom of the largest mound, there were two old glass jars with remnants of decayed mushrooms. As I looked more carefully around the area, I was astounded to find a whole site of artifacts which appeared to be 20 to 30 years old. In one area, there stood a strange shaped tent like nothing I had ever seen. A small pyramid formed the main structure and a pivotal mushroom dome formed a roof over the pyramid. The whole thing was designed with neatly tied branches and very old canvas. I could not understand the very small size of the structure as I opened the tattered flap and went inside. It was barely big enough for one person to sit down and that was it. You could not possibly have laid down. One little window cast scattered rays of light down to the floor revealing a flat stone with the words "Welcome to the Mushroom Tent" etched lightly on it.

Just outside the tent, about 30 feet away, was a fire pit area consisting of angular stones and a slate base. I would find out later that the slate held and radiated the heat to provide extra warmth. A lone, weather bleached stick was firmly rooted in the ground over-hanging the pit. A small well crafted hole was centered in the widened top of the stick. Piercing the hole was another perfected looking stick that had a rounded turning handle on one end and a sharp point on the other. The whole thing looked so delicate and masterful. To top it all off, I noticed a covered pile of wood near the pit while I was moving the leaves and moss around. Underneath a rusted cover, piles of dry branches cut at exact lengths were arranged from the smallest diameter to the largest. I had never seen anything in my life that compared to this place and its mystical order. Only after many visits to the mushroom site over four or five seasons did I come to understand its purpose and the soul who once lived or spent time there. My first experience of the pine grove though, left me completely confounded.

The quiet solitude and peace of the place brought me back often. I felt at home there after awhile and was able to let go of all the worries and pressures of daily life. I learned so much about natural harmony and the beauty of simplicity in living in the midst of pine scented breaths, white-tailed deer, horned owls, spotted hawks, gray squirrels, black bears, rabbits and delicious mushrooms. I was able to know the safe, edible mushrooms by watching the animals. They avoided the poisonous and hallucinogenic ones and so did I. Many late summer evenings would find me roasting wonderful nut flavored mushrooms over the old fire pit. I always felt the presence of a very wise soul there at the site communicating with me through the animals and the natural order of the place. I always respected the site and left it clean and exactly as I found it. For some strange reason, I felt that the special soul who constructed the site still lived there in some form.

At the college by day, I was studying the sciences, philosophy and theology, coming to know man's rational interpretations of "reality". At the same time, I was working two jobs to afford the material 'reality' expected of me by society. At the site during the evenings though, I was learning about another reality: the reality of time-lessness and truth within myself accessible only through moments of peace, solitude and respect for all life. This realm always felt more real to me than any other. I could not find God in my theology classes. I only found the historical perspective of the Church which, often times, shocked me. I tried being a part of many religious institutions but could not find God in those places... only narrow minded belief systems which left many people empty and emotionally sick. I could not find God through my parents, friends or any aspects of modern society. But I could find and did find the experience of God and the magical process of life and creation within myself by spending many private moments of solitude and reverence at the mushroom site.

CHAPTER IV

A S THE YEARS WENT BY, I found peace through a growing understanding of the drowning experience. Remembering the vision of afterlife, I came to know that I was on a journey towards understanding the message of Christ over many mountains of spiritual realization and through many valleys of emotional despair. Passing through the valleys, which were often very dark and difficult, would eventually lead to emotional growth. Like so many people from my generation, I had not known love as a child. So, I went into my adulthood and into relationships with women unable to give or accept love - (A reflection of my own state of being!) I came face to face with this problem at the age of twenty-two, two years into college. I could not go on in life without facing serious emotional issues. At the same time, I was discovering some real truth in the Christian prophesies and in the prophesies of other cultures such as the Mayan, Hindu and Chinese. The more I opened my mind through study and meditation, the more I came to see that I was living in a world on the brink of political, geological and economic chaos. I had so many questions, and I had never related well to the material culture of America which had been built on the suffering of others. I had become really upset when I learned about places like Guatemala and how the CIA kept the people there repressed in order to preserve their fronted business like United Fruit Company. The native people of Guatemala are forced to work for less than a dollar a day, harvesting fruit and vegetables on the land that was once their own, to be sent to the United States just to ensure cheap prices for bananas on the grocery shelves. My college education was exposing me to the painful realities of injustice and economic systems all over this continent – systems built on lies and treachery. I loved this country, but I could sense that a great wind of change and retribution would someday sweep over America. All of these sudden realizations, combined with the spiritual experiences that I had had up to that point in my life, brought me to the summer of '77.

Groping to find myself and my purpose in this life, I decided to give up college for awhile and joined the Peace Corps. I really wanted to reach out and give myself to the Third world struggle. I thought that the Peace Corps would be the answer... Was I ever wrong! I was assigned to go to the Micronesian Islands in the South Pacific to work in a foreman-type position in a small molding factory owned by American and other foreign investors. After looking into the position, I found out that it was their procedure to strip the Islands one by one of precious rare woods in order to make fancy molding for the rich back in the developed world. Meanwhile, the native peoples worked for starvation wages while their culture, which revolved around the trees, was destroyed. After all the trees were cut, the factory would be moved to another island leaving the people dependent on surplus food (welfare) shipped in from America. Needless to say, I turned the position down and wrote the Washington office a very angry and concerned letter about their "humanitarian" policies. I was quickly reassigned to a position in South Yemen working at a boys' orphanage. I did not know then that North and South Yemen were on the brink of communist war and the U.S. government wanted to put a few American civilians in South Yemen as political pawns. I was suspicious, though, and the suspicion grew when two Arabian men showed up in San Francisco, where I was making a short visit, and followed me everywhere I went. I had called my sister in Maine and learned that two Arabian men were *courting* her during this same time. They were buying her clothes and dinners and had offered her trips to Washington D.C. It did not take me long to figure out that my honesty with the Peace Corps had put my life in some kind of danger. I headed back to Maine immediately and went to stay with a friend who was building a cabin in a remote area. I did not have any fear about the incident, but it served to drive me further towards deep introspection about this society and where I was going.

Somewhere within my soul, there was a place I needed to go. My intense searching, my education thus far and my desire to experience nature on a more basic and primal level were all strong factors in my decision that summer to cleanse my mind and body with a long dedicated fast. I needed to find my place... my *vision* in this life. After saying goodbye to my family and friends, I headed out into the forested hills of Central Maine. There was no other path for me at the time. Something was out there for me to experience, or, rather, something was calling from within me. Even my decision to fast was really only a conscious acceptance of my destiny and the calling to experience the deeper realms of existence. My family thought that I had completely lost my mind, of course, but their grounding in life was rooted in emotional insecurity, addictive behavior and material satisfaction... the same as much of the rest of American society. I was on a different path. Their fears and condemnation had little or no effect on what I felt I needed to do.

From that point on, each day that passed left me experiencing increasingly more peace and freedom. By day, I wandered up streams and through virgin forest groves trying to keep a fix on the general location of my wandering so as not to get totally lost. This fear slowly dissolved after the fourth day as I felt a deep intuitive trust in the normally unseen world that I was starting to experience, and I somehow knew that I would not be led astray. By night, I lay in pine needle beds that were always ready, it seemed, for my weakening body. Every once in a while, I would climb to the top of a giant hemlock tree and rest for the night. At about sixty or seventy feet in the air, the top branches of hemlock trees are thick, solidly interwoven and crescent shaped. There is no way you can fall out of that natural hemlock hammock. The summer night breezes and deep crystal skies that I experienced in those hemlock tops began to open me up to a cosmic realm of consciousness. My state of being was elevated more and more each day as I deprived my material body. The spiritual aspect of myself was becoming the dominant force of my being and was reaching out for a vision and the fruit of mystical experience.

On the evening of the fifth day, I became very weak and semi-conscious. I was hungry and ate one red-topped mushroom that was growing at the base of a large hemlock that I would climb for the night. I was led to the tree, it seemed, by a raven which had been following me all day, making many different sounds and calls as if to tell me something. I could barely pull myself up through the thick branches, but, after a while, finally made it into the swaying cradle of the tree-top under the midnight canopy of sky. Something was changing in me that night. There was no fear, worry or conscious, analytical thinking... only the letting go of my separate identity to the unconscious realm.

I could have died a physical death that night and, perhaps, my individual "ego" self did. I do know that the many places I went in the spirit were real - just as real as the hemlock tree in which I lay. I remember a feeling of passing back through time. Waves of alternate white light seemed to be the conscious experiences of lives, and the moments of colored light being the unconscious or subjective experience which most people call death. Within the white light, there were glimpses of my own history, interrelated with the history of humanity. Within the moments of subjectivity, it seemed that I merged with God and universal truth. Only after hundreds and hundreds of these dawn/dusk cycles did I awake to a past life on the level of sensual experience:

I awoke climbing a stone footpath high above a radiant sea. All around me there were mountains which rose directly from the tidal currents interrupted only by very small, sandy, shell-filled coves. I could see that I was on an island, and in the distance was a vast shoreline stretching across the horizon. My name was Anathenius and the shoreline on the horizon was the western edge of Atlantis. Ahead of me on the footpath were many women and children brought here by my mother and me to escape the corrupt God-Kings of central Atlantis. I could see her small fleet of boats, silhouetted against the emerald reflection in the ocean, heading back to rescue more people. There had been rumors of war with China, and even more terrifying, the land had started shaking with constant tremors. Above me, high in the mountains, a camp had been established years earlier by my mother, Astaria, and by many others to preserve the old ways. I never made it to the camp that day, for I watched in horror as the great continent of Atlantis exploded and started sinking into the sea. I was thrown to the ground while the whole foundation of the world shook so hard as to throw all human beings off the surface of the blue star. Great clouds of ash, steam and molten rocks were enveloping me just as my mother's small fleet disappeared under a giant wave.

We are never given more pain than is possible to bear during any transitional moments between life and the afterlife... pain is an experience rooted in the material realm of feeling. The moment that the soul begins releasing the body is when the pain stops. After I saw the small fleet disappear, I went through a few short agonizing moments of gasping for air while suffering flashes of burning sensations. Soon, my soul was gone from the body of Anathenius and immersed in the fountain of light which flows eternally into all souls. With me were many others; a tidal wave of human souls rushing away from the material world as the whole continent of Atlantis was destroyed. We were all cleansed and subjected to truth's unveiling power. I was healed of my sorrow and realized my personal failures, for, at the time of my death on the island, there was a desire in my heart for a just life. There was no judgment, only the burning light of truth and the exposing to the light the level of love that I had come to understand during my previous lives on Earth. This was the determining factor in my continued evolution as a human being.

"Atlantis is gone because of the many mistakes made by both humans and their gods."

I could feel these words echo through my soul as I was transported somehow to the home of the Great Grandfather-Mother-Creator in the center of this galaxy. The Being that was before me, radiating these thoughts and words into my soul, was both male and female energy with millions of forms. Currents of magnetic feeling, deeper than love, spiraled out to every star in the galaxy, it seemed, and I wanted to merge forever into its glowing aura of creative freedom.

"Original creation in the material realm is never

without imperfection. There has always been creative freedom among the younger Creator-gods as it was for me. The creative process in this galaxy is reflected from the center here all the way down through the generations of Creator-gods into human beings. Each Creator or star has its own system of planetary being but is also a part of a larger system of stars which is part of even a larger system. When you look into the night sky on Earth, Anathenius, do you not see millions of stars? Every one of these points of light is a realm of my children and all their children's children. Your creator is the whole of your sun-star, planets and all beings conscious and unconscious within your solar system, including Earth. Earth is the third planet that your Creator has attempted conscious development on in the material realms of your solar system. There was a planet between the planets you call Mars and Jupiter but that planet was destroyed accidentally after your Creator manifested conscious existence on Mars. The planets were cooling over time just as Earth is now. Mars cooled faster than Earth, just as Venus is now beginning to cool. Your Earth, Anathenius, will eventually lose its ability to support human beings in the material realm. Twice your Creator has had to transport itself closer to the sun and thus, a more spiritual link with the center of the galaxy here. There were four terrestrial planets with solid mass in the beginning but now there are only three. The planet that you call Venus will be the final chapter of your evolution and journey in that solar system. Your Creator planted its own being first on Chiron, then on Mars and then on Earth.

In the material realm, itself reflected as both male and female. All experience of duality comes from one source of an evolving Creator being which embodies both the male and the female energy. As human beings evolve into the more spiritual realms of being, the male and female aspects of existence will again merge together in balanced harmony. Manifestation into the material world is only one of the paths revealed to all Creator-Gods and can be followed to find balance and eternal freedom: a state of existence that even I have not reached yet."

"Creation on your home planet, Anathenius, has expressed itself through individual human beings and through the collective whole of humanity in order to experience itself completely and to re-create on new levels and in new worlds. This is the way of this galaxy for now. You, Anathenius, must realize your part in the creative process and the expression of the Creator that is within you...that is the purpose of all human life on Earth. Your Creator, who is my grandchild, is learning just as I, too, am learning, to find the realms of being and balance that escape all cycles of destruction. When you exist on the shores of Earth, you exist as an expression of the Creator developing progressively towards more universally creative power. Many of your brother and sister souls are free from the cycles of destruction on the individual level but far more are bound in the cycles of destruction which comes from the abuse of creative power. But in the collective sense, Anathenius, all human souls together are the mind and spirit of your Creator who is always trying to develop to higher levels of cosmic creation. Only the creative thoughts of love and peace expressed by human souls will move towards the realms of eternal creative freedom. In the realm of matter, in which the Earth is manifested, there is the world of feeling and emotion. This world has always been a difficult place to evolve creation, but it's a special world that can offer extreme pleasure and fulfillment or extreme anguish. These are the worlds, though, that produce the highest states of consciousness and thus eternities. Eternalness comes only from long, involved acts of creation of which all existence in this galaxy is a part."

"Destruction in this world is a part of this process for now, Anathenius, as you will come to understand. Your Creator is in both material and spiritual form now and must finish and fulfill a process of creation started long ago and which is a part of a whole galactic and universal process. There will be many times in the future when your Creator will focus and emerge in certain individuals through advanced consciousness so as to direct and re-direct the creative process. And there will emerge, in time, an image of perfection through love who will truly direct the tides of Earth experience to a point of tremendous global destruction and change in order to promote a more love-based consciousness.

Your *Creator,* in all its male and female forms, has found that love is the highest state of being in the material realm and is the key to all universal creation. This is very good for the collective soul of humanity. If your Creator had chosen one of many other paths of creation that exist in the material realms, the road to eternal being could have been much more difficult in the long run and perhaps never found. In this case, your Creator could have possibly experienced total destruction of itself and returned to the collective realm of universal dust and nothingness to be re-created. Your Creator is re-living the experience of mortal responsibility again as in earlier attempts and the world you just left proved to be too short of the desired love consciousness and global harmony. The mistakes made have been in finding the balance between both the male and female aspects of existence on Earth, as these aspects of your Creator are extremely magnified in the material realm of duality. There must be a perfect state of harmony between the god and the goddess – male and female – as you will relate to personally in future lives. Carry with you this knowledge as I am able to share the truth of your God with the great, great grandchildren of mine, but I can never intervene in the creative process of your world directly unless total destruction of my grandchild would become evident to Me. Go now... back to Earth and the lives you must live, Anathenius, and may you always be aware of these things and the God and Goddess within you."

I come to you Grandmother Creator...
*   in truth and in Love*
I ask only for light in my path
through the shadows and illusions
*   of my undeveloped self.*
Please guide me here.........
Please allow the beauty and purpose of this soul
to be understood.
In the name of Jesus,
and all the great lights
*   of humankind......Amen*

CHAPTER V

IT WAS NEARLY THREE MONTHS before I broke the long fast and solitude that summer of '77 and began to re-ground myself back into a busy life of trade work and college. But when remembering the summer of fasting and visionary past life experience on a warm February afternoon in Amalia, and having just recently been flooded with an unconscious impulse during the mysterious illness and stay in the Taos hospital, I was not completely sure if maybe the material reality of my life was the *dream* and the mystical experiences were the reality of my being. After all, I thought, it was a mystical dream that led me here to Amalia and now, down on the valley floor, there rested the totem: the manifestation of Red Feather and another realm. This manifestation had changed my life and my family's life forever and I wondered about the ultimate purpose of the totem. A growing feeling in my heart was telling me that it was almost time to head for Arizona with the great pine eagle.

Revived and energized from a hard climb and quiet meditation in the mountains surrounding the valley of Amalia, I got up and descended back to the banks of the Rio Costilla river and to the small adobe house where my family was waiting for me. All the way down I thought about the difference between the conscious and unconscious state of being and decided that the reality of my life and present journey was something I just could not fully understand. I just accepted it and was secretly thankful for the near-death and past life experiences as they had begun to merge together with rational illumination in my mind. I was developing a penetrating insight and expanding understanding of human drama here on Earth. I was beginning to realize that there was a very deep connection between the teachings of Christ and Native American cultures. Christ emerged in the Middle Eastern culture but taught, healed and prophesied to Central and North American cultures for many, many years, some 1,950 years ago. I did not know then, but I would soon come face to face with the legacy of Christ in one of the most remote and isolated Indian tribes in North America.

While hiking down the mountain side, I noticed a beautifully shaped white stone or something lying in my path ahead. I was amazed to find that it was a large sea shell and was very well preserved. How did a beautiful shell like this get to the elevation of 9,000 feet I wondered. It was a good omen and I would keep it for my medicine bag. Faint echoes of children playing guided me home as it was getting dark now. Soon I would have to leave my family for awhile. I knew that the rest of this journey with Red Feather had to be taken alone.

Later that evening after supper, I noticed Jessie in the kitchen busy cooking muffins and cookies. The counters were covered and she was packing up some containers with her baked goods and other foods. I asked her what she was doing, as I had not talked to her yet about my increasing feeling about leaving with the totem. As it turned out, I did not have to talk with her about it. She had dreamed the night before that I had to go. She knew it was time and just did what she could to help me get ready without questions or hesitation. It was an experience of inner knowing that we shared together that night. It was the first time since I had known Jessie that she did not express any fears or insecurities. Even though our relationship was shaky at times and our paths would soon part forever, I felt a special warmth and love with her that night which I'll never forget. Somehow the God in me and the Goddess in her was alive, and when we made love, we united into one creative expression of love energy transcending the material duality of the male and female bodies. I laid awake most of the night, as visions of Atlantis sinking crossed my inner sight and with the words of the Great Grandfather-Mother of creation echoing in my heart.

I wondered about death and about the places that I had experienced that had no relationship to time and space in the material world. The afterlife experience and many of the mystical visions and unconscious memories were more real to me than most of my conscious life. I had always struggled to find peace and understanding in the conscious realm, but it was different in the 'spiritual' realm. Peace and understanding just existed as a sort of base level. Travel in that realm was unrestricted and time was not the same. Even today, I can remember the vision of Atlantis sinking as if it was happening right in front of me. It is as if the long fast and the openness it created within my soul removed the rational barriers that blocked my deep unconscious memories. Or it could have been that I tuned into the superconscious and collective mind of humanity. Whatever the case be, I knew that there was growing unconscious force behind my life with some kind of direction. I was nervous and anxious that night. How would the next few days unfold? What right did I have to bring a strange totem pole onto a Native American reservation? Why couldn't I just forget the whole thing and sell the totem in Taos or Santa Fe? I guess I was really afraid of the future for the first time since my drowning 20 years earlier. It was the unknown and the unexplainable factors about the purpose of the totem that fostered apprehension. But like so many times before, I ended up trusting fully the Creator and Divine Will.

It was February 27, 1991. Dawn in the high valley of Amalia this time of year is cold, crisp but inspiring. My hands numbed with cold while securing the final ropes but I did not care. All of the fear and apprehension that I had felt the night before had vanished in my dreams. I was excited to think the totem would find its home, and my burden of caring for it and transporting it would be lifted. After giving Jessie and the boys loving assurance that I would be home soon, I pulled up onto the narrow canyon road and headed south and west. Mule deer and small herds of elk were feeding on last fall's alfalfa as December's snow was awash in the Rio Grande heading for the gulf.

There are times when I go for months and even years so busy and progressively working that I forget about certain spiritual and mystical experiences that were, at one time, overwhelming. Often, it takes years to assimilate the mysteries and truths of those experiences into my conscious mind. There are times, though, that my thoughts are flooded with dreams and visions remembering and re-living the times of openness to the normally unconscious realms. The drive to Arizona was one of the latter times. So often in the past I had repressed my strong mystical side for everyday society does not relate well to the unknown and irrational.

My family, especially my father, had ridiculed and condemned me during and after my fast. Condemnation of this type goes back for two thousand years in Western civilization. The political-religious leaders of Christianity never favored those who were open to nature and the mysteries of life. Instead, they feared such nonconformists and usually put them to death. My theological studies in college had made me aware of extensive condemnation of any mystical experience. I had quickly grown past any fear of social or family ridicule though, and was following my heart and the direction which all souls can find within. The real message of Christ's life and teachings was what mattered to me - not the institutionalization of fear and guilt. I could never tell my sons that they were *sinners*. They are beautiful human beings, as all children are born. I could only foster their inner beauty and creative potential. The Creator is found within our souls and not in massive stone cathedrals or in the dark confession booths of closet alcoholics. As I became enlightened about the history of the Church through study and research, I became resentful and ashamed of all the terrible condemnation of what is pure, natural and truly good. A great conspiracy against the common person and nature I thought. But I was free from it all.

Whose idea was it, I wondered, to create a religious patriarchy centered around sexual repression? People need codes of healthy morality, not ideas of guilt and sin in relationship to the beautiful union of woman and man. Sex in human beings long ago developed into more than procreation. It became an expression of the divine, cosmic act of creation - the union of thought and matter... idea and material... the god and goddess as one (reflecting in the image of) the original act of creation here on Earth in the material realm. One can transcend the material world, as true mystics have done for ages, and experience the divine through forms of spiritual ecstasy. The souls who take this path are always the souls who have found a perfected balance of the God and Goddess within themselves, and thus the higher levels of divine creativity are open to them.

"There will emerge, in time, an image of perfection through love who will truly direct the tides of history." I remembered those words from the great Creator Being at the center of the Milky Way, our galaxy. There have been infamous leaders and powerful kings and queens in historical times but Christ was different. His way of life and love was meant to be a great example for all human souls to find everlasting peace. Christ was centered and balanced between both the material and spiritual realms: the Goddess and the God within. I had come to understand that all of his message that has been transmitted down to the present and all of the historical expressions of humanity's relationship to the divine in Christianity was interpreted scripturally by an extremely patriarchal, male -dominated culture. This is why the *Father and Son* images were so strong. But Christ went against the norm of his day. Basic male attitude then, in the early Christian-Roman times, was egotistical, immoral, greedy and condemning of women and it still is much the same today.

Jesus Christ appeared and took a stand against these behaviors because they were destructive behaviors upon the individual and collective souls of humanity. Our Creator became fully realized in the Being of Christ. We are all expressions of our Creator, but both male and female aspects of our Creator profoundly emerged through Christ. The female side of Christ was well developed. He healed with the mystical powers so feared by the philosophers and church fathers. The church has tried to stamp out or control the goddess cults and the sisterhoods of women all through the ages. Mystical experience was always associated with the goddess. Women, by nature, have a relationship with the unconscious, mysterious realms such as the magical and herbal (nature) healing power of life. Christ stood up for women. "He that is without sin among you, let him first cast a stone at her." There were no stones cast. It was this powerful expression of love that has been a directing force for humanity even though the church has often-times used the name of Christ to consolidate its own political and financial power. Christ emerged, or better said, the Creator emerged in an image of perfected love to tell us that we all are of God, in God and expressions of the Divine in both the female and male form.

In reality, Christ did not change the tide of western history two thousand years ago as much as one might speculate. The Roman political force, armed with philosophy of individualized reason developed from the Greeks, as well as the idea of man being separate from nature, continued to shape history after the death of Christ. The Roman-Judaic power incorporated or destroyed the nature cults, seasonal and agricultural rituals, most all occult and astrological wisdom and the undying message of love implanted by Christ. It is the continued faith in the prophecy of Christ's return some-day here on Earth that has changed many souls and will powerfully redirect the course of humanity in the near future as modern civilization continues to unravel. I had come to understand and believe in this prophecy. This understanding did not come only through my studies of the Christian Revelation and my mystical experience of Christ, but through my growing awareness of all the many Native American cultures that had experienced Christ two thousand years ago and had developed similar prophesies about the coming of great Earth changes and spiritual purification. I wondered if maybe the seeds of new ages were planted long in advance of the actual new age as to allow a well-rooted germination period of new creative energy and purpose. It surely appeared that the seed of love evident in Christ's message was planted on both sides of the globe, but that they germinated in different ways. In Europe, the message of Christ was institutionalized and often subverted to the wills and desires of men. These institutions were unnatural and thus suppressed humanity's sacred and ritualistic connection to nature.

On the continent of North America, many Native cultures preserved the simple qualities of his message like love, peace and humility. Anyone who has ever studied the cultures of American Indians, I thought, could never deny this truth. There were cultures in Central and South America that also preserved the message of Christ and reflected the Divine in their societies. The Mayan peoples especially, worshiped Christ. They called him QUETZALCOATL. Even now, their descendants, like the Hopi, wait for the "Second Coming".

Late afternoon found me at Window Rock, Arizona... gateway to Navajo Land. Continuous day-dreaming, interrupted only by occasional glances back to check the totem position, had made the trip, thus far, seem short. I rested for a while at Window Rock and marveled at time's creation in stone. Through the *window*, Navajo land stretched for hundreds of miles. I would have to travel many of these miles to reach the Hopi Reservation. The totem looked different this afternoon. It glowed with a sharp brilliancy as never before. There was something very spooky about that totem, I thought. Sometimes I felt as though it were alive waiting patiently for me to see its purpose. It suddenly dawned on me: I had never seen this totem stood up. Surely this eagle would be happier on top of the totem, twenty feet in the air!

CHAPTER VI

A S IF IN MAGICAL FLIGHT, the huge eagle totem sailed the high desert air behind my truck. Past the monstrous cranes of destruction in Navajo uranium mines, the totem glided silently by like a secret visitor to this material dimension. When I stopped every couple of hours or so to stretch or to get fuel, it seemed that the face of Red Feather on the totem was more alive looking out over the destroyed land and over every town I went through. The expression on Red Feather's face seemed to change too, but never was it devoid of seriousness and patient commitment. Following the setting sun, we moved further west across the Navajo reservation finally reaching the Hopi's First Mesa at dusk.

Where would I stop, I wondered, and how would I find the group or person that represented the tribe as a whole? I decided to leave the latter worry until the next morning and concentrate on finding a secluded place to pull the truck and totem off the road. I was tired and could barely keep my eyes open. Finding a secluded spot on Hopi land was no easy job. You could see for miles in every direction from the top of the mesas and there were no places to turn off the highway through the winding curves and steep grades connecting the stone islands. Before I could realize it, I was driving up through the ancient cliffs towards Third Mesa. I couldn't believe that people actually lived atop these dry stone plateaus. It was nearly dark now, and I felt a strange and mystical feeling while approaching Third Mesa. It was a certain feeling I'd had many times before. There was a strong sense of comfort and security that everything would work out, for I had an inner faith that higher forces of good were at work ahead of me and were taking control of my journey. Just as this realization settled into my mind, I spotted a rest area near the top of Third Mesa. I pulled off the highway onto a small plateau area over-looking Second Mesa and the southwestern sky. I could see for hundreds of miles, it seemed, to the ends of the Earth. No wonder the Hopi people settled here. All of the struggles and difficulties of surviving this harsh arid country were surely worth the price of eternal skies.

Almost eight years had passed since I had first dreamt about the totem and this journey. And now, as I drifted into the semi-conscious doorway of sleep and dreamtime, I wondered why - why was I here? There were no trees for miles around. The totem laid on the trailer, silhouetted and in stark contrast to the cliffs and giant boulders which were as old as time itself.

I had been asleep only moments when I was awakened by voices and vibrations on the trailer. Before I could turn around to look, two people knocked on the window of the truck wanting to speak with me.

"Where did you come from," they asked, "and where did you get this eagle pole?"

It was a long story, I thought. They would likely think I was a crazy man if they knew the truth. But the truth was the only answer I had. I stepped out of the truck to find a half-dozen people or so standing on the trailer touching and looking at the totem. The full moon cast a glowing light that night, causing the totem's colors to be alive and vibrant. After a few solemn moments, one of the group asked me again...

"Where did you come from?"

As best as I could, I briefly related to them the dream and how, for many years, I had worked creating the totem and preparing for the journey.

Again, there was a passing solemn moment. The group of people which consisted of two native Hopi men and four Anglo men about my age talked among themselves for a moment. Then the younger Hopi man introduced himself to me, never telling me his name, but by reaching for my hand and looking into my soul.

"My Uncle," he spoke, "has come here tonight to offer prayers for tomorrow's ceremony." He gestured to the other Hopi, an elderly man. "He wants to know about this totem. What did you mean by carving these symbols here?"

The Hopi spokesman pointed to the middle of the log where I had carved an eclipse symbolized by various angles and arrows pointing to other places on the totem. Above the eclipse, there was a carving of the Earth with a giant crack, splitting the planet in two. From the core streamed a river of scarlet red, representing a spirit which then transformed into, or became, the great Chief... staring out of the log with tremendous and uncanny power. I told the spokesman and all of the group that I did not know what the symbols meant nor did I understand the meaning of the totem, nor why I had been guided to the Hopi land. I had just followed the direction given to me in the dream.

Again there was silence, not to be broken until the Elder Hopi man stepped towards me and spoke.

"It is the prophecy of our people that this eclipse will soon come, marking the beginning of purification time."

These were the only words spoken by the elder Hopi that night and during the following days. But, standing in his presence then, and again during later meetings, a deeper, spiritual form of communication took place. Somehow he spoke with his heart. I always felt as though he knew everything about me. He knew why I was there and understood fully the totem. Any verbal communication between us was done through the younger Hopi man who acted as his spokesman. It was he who spoke next.

"Come with us to my house. We are having a meeting."

Upon entering the younger Hopi man's house, I was led to a central room with a large table. Seated at the table were seven or eight people and others stood behind in the shadows. Small kachina dolls lined up on shelves dressed the walls, and, through a beamed archway, I could see a Hopi woman making coffee and preparing food. I was surprised to see so many Anglo men, all about my age, gathered in this room. I waited in silence. It was not for me to speak or ask any questions, for I felt out of place and nervous. While we were served coffee, bread and mutton, one of the Anglo men introduced everyone to me. Three of the group were camera people and producers from New Mexico Public Television. They had come to film the Clan Elder, whom I had met earlier, as he would speak about the Hopi prophecies for one last time the following morning. He and the group who met me had come down to perform a small prayer ceremony where I had pulled off the road. They called it Prophecy Rock and the Clan Elder would speak there in the morning.

Suddenly I felt deep chills pulse up and down my spine as I was beginning to realize that it was by no accident that I had been brought to this remote reservation and on this particular night. It was as though the totem was magically placed at Prophecy Rock just moments before the prophecy ceremony. I started to get weak and nauseous as I suddenly felt like I had no control over my life. I had been used like a tool by some higher force to fulfill some mystical prophecy that I didn't even understand. Trying to calm down, I grasped my chair and held tight. The wood was real, wasn't it?

The hot coffee burned my throat and I reaffirmed my individuality.

Finally, I was formally introduced to the younger Hopi man. Dr. Chet Snow, a writer and one of the Anglo visitors, introduced him as Francisco. It was Francisco's house we were in and it was his wife who had served us earlier. She now stood in a dark corner paying deep attention to everything said.

"How did you know about Prophecy Rock?" asked Francisco. He was serious, so serious that I felt as though I may have done something wrong.

"I have never been here before," I said. "I came over three thousand miles from Maine, on the Atlantic coast."

I told them about settling in Amalia to rest and take care of my family.

"I arrived tonight by no plan or conscious reason. I just knew I had to come."

Again I related the story of the dream and how I had struggled to get the totem to this place tonight.

"I never really understood any of it. I just followed the spirit of the dream and the totem."

I could tell that Francisco and some of the Anglo men were a little shook up and shocked at the sudden turn of events, but no one there that night was more shook up than me.

As the night went by, I learned more and more about the people gathered in Francisco's house and why they were there. It was very strange. Every single person other than the film crew had just been suddenly led there to Third Mesa. A lot of questions were asked, but the Clan Elder just stared past us all as if we were already part of the past. He knew... I could tell. He had no questions. It was up to me and the others to just be at peace and accept the higher purpose of it all. I told Francisco that I was tired and wondered if it was all right to sleep in my truck already parked at Prophecy Rock. He invited me to sleep in his home but he understood my desire to be near the totem until morning.

I guess what I really needed was just to be alone for awhile in order to digest all that had happened that evening and to keep balanced in the reality of *my* life. Somehow, the truck represented my grounding. It was my connection with my family, my past and the material world. I never feared the power of God nor the power of higher, spiritual forces that were so strongly at work around me on Hopi land. But I had never really thought about a total merge into higher realities. Back at the truck, I was not alone. Two other trucks had parked near me and I could see the faces of two men illuminated by a small camp fire. "Maybe I can just climb into the truck and sleep without their noticing me," I thought, for I really needed my own space for awhile. Not to be... Within minutes they approached me with questions about the totem.

High above the stone mesas, the full moon was casting its mystical light, softly bathing the rocky landscape and allowing the unconscious aspects of human existence a short realm of freedom. After finally drifting off to sleep, I had many dreams. The most vivid one, by far, was the *dancing stones.*

I dreamed I was watching a large circle of stones alive in a ceremonial dance. The stones were rectangular, about six feet tall and two feet wide, dancing upright within a ring of larger protective stones that were moving clockwise. Each circle of stones was smaller and smaller and within each other until there was just one stone in the middle. I remember vivid colors of red, brown and yellow as each circle of dancing stones was a different color and going in alternate directions. It was a powerful scene. I felt as though I was witnessing an ancient ceremony of creation itself. Even in the dream, I was aware somehow of my separate identity and could feel my soul being energized by the experience of the *dancing stones*. But then, something happened to the circle movement of the ceremony: It stopped. And the life was gone! I could see that the center stone was gone also, and that was why the whole beautiful and powerful dance was disrupted.

I would come to realize, after a few days with the Hopi people, that my dream very much represented the condition of the tribe. The center stone represented their spiritual center: the core of values, beliefs, ways of life that unified the whole circle or family of souls. Those stones were the souls of Hopis and the perfect dance represented a time long ago, before the Spanish and Anglos arrived. The Spanish were very effective in replacing or destroying the center stone of the various native cultures they encountered as they marched both north and south from Central America.

As the first hints of dawn sparkled and glowed on the eastern horizon, I lay awake and rested in my truck. The *dancing stones* had left a very deep mark in my experience of the Hopi people which unfolded in the following days. Even now, three years later, I feel the power of the ceremonies past and the wholeness of a well balanced and centered culture. Only in the dream though... only in the dream...

CHAPTER VII

IN THE TWILIGHT OF DAWN, I lay restlessly awake, anxious to learn more about the Hopi people and present to them the eagle totem. I wondered about my purpose here in the unfolding drama on top of Third Mesa. Who were all of these non-native people gathered together today to learn about the Hopi prophesies? I had not come for this purpose, but yet I had become a part of a powerful revelation. Later that morning we all were invited back to Francisco's house. I found myself sitting in the background listening to everyone talking in turn about why they were there.

Dr. Snow, who is a noted para-psychologist and successful author, talked with the group about his new book. For over 15 years, he and other psychological researchers and hypnotherapists had catalogued thousands of hypnotic progressions into the future. Subjects had been taken from all over America and Europe, chosen from all walks and classes of life. They were progressed into the future with the help of hypnotism. All of the people progressed were asked during the mild trances to relate what they saw and how they felt. Nearly every person saw the same thing: The Earth had changed dramatically and a large portion of humanity had perished. When asked to look down on the Earth from above, almost everyone progressed had a hard time recognizing the continents because great geological upheavals had taken or were taking place. Much of modern civilization had been disrupted or destroyed - people had gathered in certain areas around the globe that were relatively safe and high above sea level. Almost all of the subjects saw the weather patterns in the future dramatically different from what they are now.

Dr. Snow had heard of the Hopi prophecies about a time of Earth purification which would be accompanied by great upheavals and geological destruction. He had come to the Hopi people to learn more about their prophecies as they correlated directly to his research. I liked Dr. Snow very much. The short time I had to talk with him was full of intense revelation. He was a scientist to the core. Only after hundreds and hundreds of future progressions did he finally accept the fact that a great planetary change was in order for humanity. It was then, after hearing the same account of global destruction, that he began to investigate the prophecies of many cultures from around the world.

Traveling with Dr. Snow was another interesting man. His name was John, a helicopter pilot who had flown in Vietnam. John was a quiet man, but somehow he facilitated group feelings and interesting conversation. I came to find out later that John was a psychologist and hypnotherapist when he wasn't flying people around in Alaska during the summer months. I felt great compassion for John. He was a wounded soul. I suppose anyone who was forced to be a part of the napalm bombing of countryside villages in Nam that gave refuge to so many women and children would never be totally stable or whole. But John was trying. It was through his service to others, his facilitation of healing and psychological release in others that he himself was healing. I wondered how many wounded souls have come back from the Far East having to deal with the type of pain that John still carried.

Rick, David and Scarlet were movie production artists from Albuquerque, representing New Mexico Public Television. They had come to do a special on

Native American philosophy and prophecies, and they had been assigned to film the Clan Elder's prearranged message about the Hopi prophecies and the coming Earth changes. It would be the last time that he would speak to the outside world about them. There would be no more warnings from the Fire Clan Elders.

"If mankind was so hell bent on destroying Mother Earth, then let the Earth changes begin."

The Hopi people have recorded great Earth changes on stone tablets and stone cliffs for thousands of years. They also still have strong oral transmission of mankind's moral history and creation myths. During the meetings at Francisco's house, I learned much about the traditional Hopi beliefs and prophecies. The current moral breakdown of humanity, the greed and the self-destruction are of no surprise to the Hopi. They have a strong historical memory about the world that existed before this one in which mankind was overtaken by evil and discontent. That world was destroyed, leaving remnants of cultures that were guilt-ridden and struggling on the brink of survival for many years. The same account of global destruction caused by humanity's moral degeneration is told by the Mayan Indians. Dr. Snow read to the group some passages from his book, written after years of research into both Mayan and Hopi creation stories. Some of the Mayan myths are identical to Old Testament myths and Dr. Snow had found similar accounts of creation and re-creation in cultures all over the world. Every single myth of past global destruction from every single culture he researched attributed great Earth changes to disharmony within the animal kingdom or disharmony and moral decadence within the human kingdom. Stories of the *great flood* are the most common, but destruction by fire and water have more than once come hand in hand throughout the ages.

We talked for hours about mythological and historical accounts of past global change. It seemed that everyone there had some piece of a prophetic puzzle and somehow the totem fit into the purpose of it all on some deep mystical level. I was getting to know almost everyone there and was curious to learn more about the two fellows that stayed at the turnout in their trucks as I had done the night before. Their names were Allen and Zolanda.

Allen was from Arizona. He had come to Hopi land hoping to meet the elders and learn about their mysteries. He was dead set on getting into the their Kiva ceremonies. He could not understand why the Hopi people did not respect his self-importance and just hand over their sacred stone tablets to him for inspection. He was an impatient sort with an untamed ego, but I liked Allen and felt a special bond with him just the same. I spent the next three days trying to subtly teach him to focus on developing the female, intuitive, side of his nature and to stop trying to force himself into a world which would always be closed to him. Too much of the sacred ways and sacred knowledge of Native Americans had been trespassed upon and invaded already. Exploitation had to stop somewhere, and sacred traditions needed to be left alone to remain sacred and accessible to only those souls who could understand and preserve them.

Then there was Zolanda, also known as Dr. Cornelius van Dorp, from New Zealand. He had recently met Allen in Sedona, Arizona, and had felt compelled to travel with him to Third Mesa. Zolanda was, by far, the most interesting and *aware* soul amongst all the Anglo men gathered there in the late February of 1991. Zolanda and I were brothers-in-time. We could read each other's mind it seemed, and we had many things in common. He had left his country medical practice in New Zealand to travel through the southwest of America and eventually end up in Central Mexico. His goal was to witness the total eclipse of the sun later that summer when it was expected to be directly over most of the sacred Mayan temple sites and much of the Yucatan. His research about the Hopi people had taught him that they were possible descendants of the Mayan and he was hoping that Hopi Elders would reveal some information about the importance of such a spectacular eclipse. He was shocked to see the image of great eclipse taking place on the eagle totem I had brought. What did the eclipse mean for humanity? Was it the end of some great cycle? Did the Mayan Indians of so long ago understand the large eclipse cycles that are still being discovered by modern astronomers?

Zolanda was a scientist by nature. A musician and writer he was... with a deep and passionate need to experience life to the fullest. He was an extremely aware man who loved the Earth, its land and its seas. He had found his soul purpose during a six month stay in Antarctica while serving for Green Peace. He was on a quest for truth and knowledge. He was on a quest for spiritual understanding and mystical power, for he believed that he could not be effective in changing the destructive course of humanity without first achieving these abilities. Months of sea duty with Green Peace, chasing Japanese dragnetters, had left him frustrated and weary, but he was determined to never give up his quest.

Allen had decided to join up with Zolanda for the summer and travel to Central Mexico for the July eclipse. Zolanda was convinced that this particular solar eclipse marked the real turning point for humanity: a time for human beings to be sure of their motives and spiritual direction. Francisco would verify this belief later that afternoon as he interpreted for us the meaning of the symbols on the totem as the Elders had directed. I was both amazed and shocked as I increasingly realized that a powerful hidden message had been somehow carved into the totem through my hands. Red Feather was now speaking to me and others gathered there through the Hopi interpreters. Red Feather was also speaking to the Hopi people, telling them to respect and have faith in their own prophesies. Like most Native American Tribes these days, they were a divided people slowly being forced away from traditional beliefs and slowly being forced off their native land.

A high quality coal had been found by miners years earlier up on Black Mesa. Uranium and other metals also lie under all the Hopi Mesas. Many of the tribe had sold out to the Federal Government in the sense that they were allowing large scale mining while accepting money and political guidance from Washington. This had caused a tremendous rift between the new political Hopis and the traditional Hopis who believed that it was wrong to destroy their land. Things had changed too fast. Without the strong religious and ceremonial connection to their culture, many young and middle age Hopi people were a-drift in drug and alcohol abuse.

Down on Second Mesa, there was a new school and a new police station. In front of the police station were six new police cars. A new jail was the central feature in the new station along with the latest subversion technology. "This is progress," said Washington, "a giant step towards real civilized living." One of the saddest things for me though, was the total disrespect for the land that seemed wide spread among the *new* Hopi people. Trash, broken bottles and cans were everywhere. Many areas on Second Mesa were littered to death. I couldn't believe my eyes the first morning I had a chance to look around. I could feel, too, a general sense of emotional depression among the *political* Hopi people. They were not happy and were suffering from the destruction of their spiritual culture. There were some who lived in both worlds - they were the strong ones-artists and healers mostly. Francisco was an artist who lived in both worlds. He saw the value of both worlds if a balance and harmony could someday be found.

Later that evening, just before sunset, we all gathered around the trailer which cradled the totem in hopes of understanding its hidden meaning.

"This totem has come as a warning to Hopi people that the prophecies cannot be ignored or forgotten. The eclipse symbolizes great changes coming to the four directions of Earth experience."

The translator pointed to the various arrows and markings on the totem as he spoke.

"This sun image above the medicine bag represents all that is sacred and cannot ever be lost. The Creator would never allow such a thing to happen. Up here, the Earth is splitting open to reveal the spirit of a great leader emerging out of destruction and change. His name is not important for his spirit is clothed in many forms, depending on the culture in which he appears. He is the Chief of peace and love and he will have great power over the evil and greedy forces on Earth. Above the Chief's head emerges an eagle, the great thunderbird of dignity and power. Many Hopi people and many people in your culture wait patiently for the return of the Great Chief. He is coming soon after the great purification of Mother Earth and of human souls."

The last gold ray from the setting sun vanished softly away as did the translator's voice. As I sat by the warm fire Zolanda had made that night at Prophecy Rock, I had visions of the "Great Chief" coming to Earth with armies of archangels to take control of desperate race of human beings. That is what it's going to take, I thought... intervention by divine forces. The idea of divine forces at work in the universe and here on Earth was becoming a reality for me. Many souls of my generation were being directed by this divine force and being prepared for the future. I was not the only person led here to Hopi land to be awakened.

Before I climbed into my truck for the night, I stood for awhile and looked into the face of Red Feather on the totem. Again, his face had changed. I felt peace and resolve. It had been a long journey, a long wait and struggle. But now Red Feather was awakening...

CHAPTER VIII

R ESTLESS AND FULL OF THE MANY PROPHETIC VISIONS implanted in my mind all day during the meetings, I walked along the cliff side near Prophecy Rock. It was midnight, and I had not been able to sleep. I was still having a hard time waking up to the fact that my life had been so mystically directed for the past six or seven years. It wasn't that I was harboring fear or resentment for I had absolutely no bad feelings or regrets about the whole experience starting with the first totem dream. It was just all so amazing, especially the group experience with others who had also been guided here to the Hopi Mesas. In the night shadows of moonlit rock, I found peace, calm and spiritual serenity. I could sense that thousand of generations of Hopi people had come and gone over the same foot path that I was walking. For a moment, I thought I saw someone move in the shadows, but I had experienced the many faces of 'dreamtime' before and kept walking.

Suddenly, and very quietly, a person stepped out from the shadows in front of me and spoke with a questioning tone:
"You are the one who brought the totem?... My grandfather wants you to come."

"Where is he?" I asked.

The Hopi man pointed up to the cliffs of Oriabi. The thin, middle aged man then began walking very fast up through the winding foot paths along the cliffs. In some places it was very dark as the moonlight was blocked by huge stone out-croppings. But the path was never difficult to find. It was as if a continuous magnetic current pulled my feet along and I could even close my

eyes while walking ahead. The magnetic feeling increased as each moment passed, almost lifting me up
through the rocks.

Soon we were near the top and I could see five or
six Hopi people silhouetted against the western night
sky. As I moved closer, I could see that they were dressed
in masks and ceremonial feathers, preparing to climb
down a pole-type ladder rising up out of a hole in the
level stone area that we were standing on.

"My grandfather says it's okay for you to enter the
Kiva."

The guide then motioned me down the ladder after
the other people had disappeared into the ground. Just
as the mysterious current had pulled me up the cliffs, so
too did it carry me down into the Kiva. I did not question
what had unfolded. Past mystical experience had taught
me to let go and just feel the moment without conscious
rationalization. It was a different type of *seeing*. Only
now, two years later, can I formulate the experience into
the words and structure of the English language.

The Kiva was warm and protective. Steady, low
and rhythmic breathing echoed from the center of the
Earth it seemed. The guide spoke one last time to me
before I left my ego self and merged with the oneness of
the ceremony.

"My grandfather wants to show you the beginning
of the world... the fourth world."

I remember the Native chants and songs and how,
as each moment passed, the Kiva itself dropped into
another dimension revealing a whole different world.
Suddenly I could see below and around me many different places and people. Ancient cultures from all over
the Earth were alive and thriving. Different perspectives
of the Earth and humanity long ago cascaded by and
around me, coming more and more into focus. The

colors, the stone cities, the sculptures and the healthy people…it was so beautiful. Ships on the sea and in the air carried merchants, travelers, goods and knowledge from one culture to another. There were no images of war or starvation at first, only peace and trans-cultural cooperation. Then the cascading scenes began to change. The focus increased on individuals and various social institutions of many cultures. I could see that people were not at peace nor were they as in the beginning scenes I had witnessed. They were becoming selfish and corrupt. I could see hungry and abused children abandoned in city centers. The gift of sexual bonding and union between men and women was being abused all over the world. People wanted more than they needed and society became unbalanced and decadent. Now there were wars and people were no longer healthy and vibrant for sickness and disease became common.

I could see into the heavens, too, or into some higher realm of existence. The Creator Gods were not happy. Both He and She anguished over their spiritually lost children and their failed attempt at re-creation on the blue star of Earth. They talked about the turmoil and the increasing collapse of the ideals of love, beauty and respect. Where had they gone wrong? Had they left the planet and their children too soon?… They talked about destruction; who would survive and how long would it take to heal the human drama they had created? They wondered about their parents who lived closer to the center of the galaxy. Would they be angry? Would they help them save their children?

Then I saw the world and its many cultures coming back into focus again. Thick, black clouds were on every horizon. Dust, ash and smoke arose from even the oceans as new mountain chains suddenly appeared where once there was water. Whole cities disappeared under the sea. Super hot lava collided with ice in the Atlantic while giant tidal waves swept the Pacific. Much of the Earth was flooded as the oceans took weeks to rearrange and settle back into natural shores. Walls of water one-hundred feet deep took whole populations away in some places, leaving only the stone structures.

When it was all over, I saw that many, many people had died as the global upheaval and deluge had touched every corner of the Earth. Some cultures were gone forever... only their artifacts and stone buildings remained. Everywhere there were people wandering the hillsides looking for shelter and food. People were fearful and distraught. How could their Gods have allowed this to happen? Confusion, anger and collective feelings of shame and guilt lasted for months and years among the surviving people from all cultures. Some cultures survived intact though, and redeveloped their philosophies of creation and man's relationship to the divine. Others were left broken and in desperation but they, too, slowly began to rebuild their lives, often merging with remnant souls of other distraught cultures. Stories about the disaster and about man's punishment for wicked ways flourished all over the world giving rise to a new age of recovery.

It was at this point in the ceremonial journey into the past that the scenes of Earth life vanished and the Hopi chanting and songs became a whisper in the Arizona night. My guide spoke once more as he motioned for me to follow him up the pole ladder to the desert plateau above.

"You see we live in the fourth world now. The third world had to be destroyed."

Startled, I awoke to knocking on my truck windshield. It was Zolanda.

"Jonathon... wake up." It was late. The sun was

already perched to climb the zenith.

"The third world had to be... destroyed?"

I wondered about the night before. Had I gone into the Kiva ceremony or had I gone into the dream world? Whatever be the case, I was beginning to understand the Hopi prophecy. The whole purpose of my being there on Hopi land was also beginning to unfold in my streams of understanding. I wondered about the fourth world, the world that I now stood in. Would it too be destroyed like the third world? The Hopi people, through their spiritual ceremonies and transference of their ancient history from generation to generation, have kept a window open to humanity's past. And somehow, they have a window to the future. I had many questions about the Hopi understanding of the past, present and future world but they would have to wait...

Zolanda again knocked on the window.

"Jonathon, I brought you some coffee."

The wind was damp this morning and long banks of gray-blue clouds were sailing in from the west. I sat down by the fire and stared at the dying flames.

"What are you going to do with the totem?" Allen asked.

I thought for a minute.

"I'm not sure...Perhaps I'll take it to the tribal office this morning."

Zolanda offered me a muffin from the box that Jessie had packed. It was just what my body needed and it served to ground me in the practical reality of my life and the need to fulfill my purpose with the totem and get back to my family in Northern New Mexico. I could feel the pull of their hearts and I missed them.

CHAPTER IX

FRANCISCO HAD WANTED ME TO LEAVE THE TOTEM with him at his house on Third Mesa as he felt that it belonged with the traditional minded Hopi people. Leaving it with him would have been the easiest thing to do, for I could have gotten started back for Amalia. But something in my heart told me that my responsibility with the totem wasn't over yet. The totem was a gift to all the Hopi people. Implanted into the 20-foot log was a very prophetic message that connected deeply with the Hopi prophecies of Earth purification. But yet the totem came from three thousand miles away and from the direction of a higher force. Was it meant to warn the political Hopis not to reject or ignore their own cultural heritage and spiritual prophecies? If it was, why then the Hopi people? Was the totem meant for me to awaken to a new realm of truth? Whatever be the case, I felt I needed to take the totem down to the Tribal Government offices on Second Mesa.

Following one's intuition is not always the easy path. It can often mean the need for patience and per-severance. That is exactly what it took for me to deal with the political Hopis. They wanted to know the value of the totem as a piece of art work: how much it might be worth. It was massive and beautiful, they said; but that is all they saw in it. They had no idea of its real message at first and were more than willing to accept the totem. Later that day, after a large group of people had un-loaded the totem at the "Cultural Center" on Second Mesa, Francisco and I had a chance to speak alone. I began to explain to him that my intuition had told me to leave the totem on Second Mesa. He told me to say no more and said, "It is right for the totem to be on Second Mesa. These people have forgotten the prophecies."

Back at Prophecy Rock, Allen, Zolanda and I sat by the fire, trying to dry out from the cold rain that had soaked us while unloading the totem on Second Mesa. It had been damp most of the day but now the setting sun blazed crimson holes through the eastbound clouds. In the distance were the San Francisco Peaks - white from a fresh snowfall.

As the sun slipped behind the distant peaks, a very eerie mist settled over the campsite area. Within the mist I could see the spirits of two Hopi men doing what seemed to be a simple prayer ceremony. Allen and Zolanda had climbed into their trucks for the night by now and the two translucent men in the mist had moved closer to me. The Elder man of the two stood for awhile facing eastward... then he blew some white cornmeal towards the clouds. When he was done, they both came over and sat down by the fire and did another cornmeal offering. They spoke for a few minutes in their native tongue before speaking to me. The younger man translated for the Elder as he began to speak:

"You have been brought here to learn about the Hopi Prophesies and the Hopi beliefs about today's world... the fourth world. After we came to the fourth world, we lived in peace and harmony for many, many eclipse cycles. Our ancestors developed in the arts and sciences and rebuilt the large stone cities that were left standing from the third world. There was an abundance of all things and our ancestors prospered in every way. There was peace throughout the lands and between nations because the memory of destruction by fire and water over much of the Earth was kept vividly alive in the hearts and souls of people through the stories and history preserved by the sacred time-keepers. Over time, though, our leaders became greedy and corrupt and the dark forces were entering our ceremonies. Many of our people forgot or ignored the stories of destruction and change that comes to the unjust and wicked. Then came Quetzalcoatl, the Great White Brother. It is told that he came to the earth from the great clouds over the eastern sea. He was a very wise and loving Being and a powerful healer. He could heal anyone from any sickness and even bring back our dead to life, yet there were small wounds on his hands and feet that never healed. He said he was from Venus, and that someday all souls would come to know that brilliant morning and evening star."

The younger man stopped relating the Elder's message for a moment. By this time, I was overcome with chills for I knew that the Quetzalcoatl whom the Elder was talking about was Christ. Soon, the Elder continued speaking:

"He talked of love and peace as he cared for all people no matter what position or place they had in society. This man, Quetzalcoatl had great magic. He traveled throughout the continent from the east shores to the west shores and from the north to the south performing great wonders. He helped many tribes develop laws of peace and compassion. He never condemned anyone. His powerful energy of love would just heal them. That was a great time to be alive in the 'Americas'. After Quetzalcoatl left, two or three hundred years went by without any conflicts between peoples and nations. But the cities progressively became centers of greed and corruption as the leaders demanded more of the common man's crops and crafted goods. Some of my ancestors were Mayan. Many of them banded together and traveled north to these Mesas to begin a new life free from the political corruption in the South Central areas of the continent. Life here on the Mesas was harsh and difficult at first. They had never experience winters of snow and icy winds. By the second winter, the whole tribe was facing starvation because the fall's harvest had not been good."

"It was mid-winter when Quetzalcoatl appeared to them out of the eastern dawn. He gathered the whole tribe on what is now called First Mesa. There, he asked the people to each pick up the eight small stones and set them near their feet. He then asked one of the children to take his eight stones and place them in the ground at the center place of all the people gathered. The young boy dug a small hole and covered up his eight stones. After this was done, Quetzalcoatl took a handful of tiny eagle-down feathers from a small deerskin bag and released them to the wind which was blowing to the east. Just as the feathers rose out of sight, the sun's rays burned through the clouds on the horizon and transformed the whole eastern sky into a panoramic scene of the village on First Mesa. It was as though a hole had opened up in the dawn, revealing the future of the people. The scene in the sky was not the same as life on First Mesa that winter day. Within the clouds was a beautiful and successful Hopi culture. The people were dressed in ceremonial masks and costumes celebrating the many blessings of rich harvests and happy lives. The hungry people that were watching the scene were all in awe of the magical vision and Quetzalcoatl told them that this was to be experienced in their future. Many of our sacred ceremonies which are still continued today came from the teachings of Quetzalcoatl that day as he showed my ancestors many things about living in harmony with the Earth and each other. His teachings eventually manifested into many sacred spiritual ceremonies. As the scene faded, the people screamed and shouted for joy for the stones at their feet had turned into huge ears of corn."

"Each person had two yellow, two red, two blue and two white ears of corn. The center place where the child had put his stones had been transformed into a large opening in the ground. The people gathered around the hole and looked into a large cavern hollowed out in the rock. Quetzalcoatl told them that this cavern would be a sacred meeting place where they could enter the spiritual realms of life. Then he told them to put there white ears of corn into the cavern for the future... as the white corn was sacred and would bring many spiritual blessings. Our people would never go hungry again. Quetzalcoatl related the four colors of corn to the four main aspects of human experience: body, soul, mind and the divine. Over time, the cavern became known as the Kiva; and whenever our people would enter the Kiva, they would emerge renewed and full of spirit. They would be nourished with the energy of light and creation."

"Quetzalcoatl feasted with the people and told them many stories of things past and things to come. While he talked he healed each person of sickness, cold and all ailments with only his glancing touch. One of the little children sitting in the Quetzalcoatl's lap asked him why he did not heal the piercing, half healed wounds in his palms and through his feet. He did not answer the child. He only bowed his head in silence. Later, he talked of a day when a strange people would come to our land from the east. Our land would be changed and our culture would be nearly destroyed. Not until this time would he come back to help many people go to the fifth world. He told the people, now nourished, content and warm from the ripe ears of corn, about the fifth world."

"After Quetzalcoatl left, the rest of that winter was

very good for my ancestors. Every time they would eat their corn, two more of each color would mysteriously appear. We always keep the white corn as the most sacred and, to this day, use white corn in our ceremonies and offerings. This God you call Jesus Christ is also Quetzalcoatl. We have been waiting for his return. He is the Great White Brother to us now, for when your culture came with the image of Quetzalcoatl nailed to a cross, we understood the meaning of his piercing wounds that never healed. We understood how he suffered but yet came to us with so much goodness and love. He was teacher, healer and highest of all medicine men for my ancestors. Quetzalcoatl left with promise to return at the end of a certain eclipse cycle. That day is coming soon."

With these words, the Hopi men said goodbye and left. I could not believe the story that I had just heard. It was so amazing. It was so incredible. But it was also very sad. Now, it was all starting to fit together. There was no doubt that Christ had visited the lost tribes or Native Americans after his crucifixion and Ascension. There was no doubt that I had been guided here by higher forces or by the Great White Brother himself to learn these truths. What responsibility now lay ahead for me with this knowledge? Where would my path lead me now? I knew that I'd never be the same. The story of Quetzalcoatl - the other story of Christ - had manifested new vibrations within my heart and soul. God! I wished I could experience the afterlife again now that I fully knew that it was Christ who was standing in the light.

Dawn the following morning brought an increasing easterly breeze and a parting of paths for Allen, Zolanda and me. We all agreed that someday we would be brought together again, perhaps back here on Hopi land. I stopped and said goodbye to Francisco and told him I would call after a month or so. I would come back if the Hopi People needed to move the totem or decided to stand it permanently somewhere. Within an hour or two after visiting Francisco, I was heading east through the heart of the Navajo Reservation.

CHAPTER X

SOMETIME ABOUT MIDNIGHT my eyelids became heavy, forcing me to pull off the road 50 miles or so before Window Rock, Arizona. Within minutes I was curled up sound asleep on the truck seat. I can remember successions of dreams that night and of being awakened after two or three hours by one dream in particular. It was one of those very vivid dreams that became recurring throughout the next few months. I dreamed that I was being followed by the totem as I left Hopi and Navajo territory. I was driving and the totem was hovering behind me, trying to land in the moving trailer cradle. When I would stop the truck and get out, the totem would vanish. There was this feeling that the spirit of the totem was hanging on to me even though I thought I had released myself from it with a short prayer ceremony earlier that afternoon and by finally delivering the totem to the Hopi people. I also had another feeling-one of apprehension that my journey with the totem was not over. Those feelings faded throughout the pre-dawn hours as I drove farther east and north heading for the Sangre de Cristos.

One of the most awesome and beautiful land-scapes ever to be seen on this continent, I think, is the Taos plain at Sunrise. As you come up out of the Rio Grande canyon where the road winds north along the river, you suddenly find yourself able to see for at least one hundred miles north into Colorado. Vast expanse of high plains surrounded by snow covered peaks is sliced wide open by the Rio Grande gorge. For as far as the eye can see, a giant crack in the earth's crust divides the Taos plains, creating one of the most intense natural spectacles one could ever experience. The endless sky, the great "Tao" peak, the early morning glow across oceans of fresh sage, the burning rock walls of the Taos box-canyon at dawn and the physical sensations of high altitude all come together, causing powerful feelings of humility and wonder. This planet Earth is a vast and incredible place. The Taos plain is one of those places that make you realize how insignificant one's life really is in terms of the Earth's geological time clock, and in terms of raw natural beauty.

I had read some geological information about the Taos plain and was amazed to learn that the vast expanse of reddish Earth was once the ocean floor. Even the Tao mountain top was covered with water. These are elevations of 11 to 12 thousand feet above sea level. How and when could such drastic changes have occurred on the Earth's surface?

The rising sun cast filtered rays down through mountain valleys and across my truck dashboard illuminating the small white shell that I had found a week or so earlier. It had caught my eye on the hike in Amalia before I left for the Hopi reservation. I realized at that moment that the shell had been an omen of revelations past and of revelations still to come. I had seen the great earth changes and volcanic-caused floods of the past during my fast in the Maine woods. I had watched Atlantis disappear under a lava filled sea. During the ceremony in the Hopi Kiva, I had witnessed a very similar scene: vast expanses of the continents were re-arranged, were flooded by the oceans and, eventually were reborn at new elevations. Could it really be that Earth changes of these magnitudes were in the near future? According to the Hopi Elders and according to the Christian prophesies, these changes would become a reality sooner than later. Not a moment too soon, I thought. It seemed to me that mankind had again regressed to a corrupt and desperate state of being in terms of the global society. There was no doubt in my mind that I was being educated about these matters by a higher force, both in the mystical reality and in the material reality. For what reasons, though, was still something that I couldn't fully comprehend.

As I turned off the main highway and drove along the narrow road which followed the Rio Costilla up into Amalia, I remember my experience of the Great Grandfather-Grandmother Creator during my long fast in 1977. It suddenly dawned on me that many Native American tribes have conceptions of a Great Grandfather-Grandmother Creator as the "center stone" in their spiritual philosophies. Even the Hopi people spoke of such great spiritual Elders in the heavens. Could it really be that human beings were children of such a Creator who lives even closer to the great center of this galaxy where the Great, Great Grandfather-Grandmother of Creators dwells? After all, the first words of the Bible speak of man and woman being created in the image of God. We have children. We have parents and grandparents. Who can say that our God or Creator has no creator? One could question further and ask, "Does the Great Creator at the center of this galaxy have a creator at the center of the universe?" I would venture to believe this to be the case… the ultimate theological truth. All Native peoples around this planet who did not follow the path of Western individualization and who did not place the mind and pure reason as the highest human ability over intuition believed in a hierarchy of creators. Human existence is a reflection of the universal process of existence. Human beings are potential creators on even more elevated conscious and cosmic levels. We are children - so very young and sometimes lost in power struggles and greedy games. But what is our ultimate destiny? There is only one answer, I thought. Human experience on Earth is not without universal purpose. We are meant to create our worlds, our children, our dreams and our peace and happiness. The world will not create these things for us. We are meant to learn responsibility for our creations. As we fulfill our responsibilities with our children, our lives and our dreams, we transcend the material levels towards more spiritual levels of experience. And within our souls we are all connected to the **ONE** Great Creator in the center of the Universe and beyond. Every single culture in every historical time has felt this connection. Every single person, at one time or another, has felt this connection within his/her heart and soul.

It has always amazed me how people transfer jealousy and insecurity into their ideas about God or the Divine. It's a scary thought for many people, especially for people in power, to think of a possibly higher God beyond their limited ideas. It has always amazed me, too, how so many people have fallen for the great patriarchal myth which, all too often, placed women and the matriarchal aspects of existence on a lower and less respected level. Women were related to evil in Christianity. Women were blamed for taking the "forbidden fruit" in the Garden of Eden. Remember always, I thought, that a male dominated society wrote this myth and a male dominated society has translated this myth many times during the past two thousand years. Perhaps we need new myths for the coming ages - new or more accurate conceptions of our Creator. Perhaps we need to learn from the Native American philosophies about harmony and balance between idea and matter, male and female and human and Earth. I had come from a very imbalanced culture which has all kinds of ideas about truth and freedom. I was learning though, that all these ideas of truth and freedom were within a larger conception of reality which may not have much ultimate truth nor value to the real human condition and human purpose here on Earth. Perhaps now humankind was awakening to new realms of understanding. I surely hoped so.

Awakening to new realities does not come easy, though, for individuals nor for humanity as a whole. Often a sudden major change, tragedy or upheaval has to happen in one's life before one can let go of old conceptions and ideas and embrace the new or more relevant truth. Often times the more relevant or higher truth is the underlying truth all along but was not seen nor realized. All of the Native American creation myths that I have encountered or read about tell the stories of past worlds which have been destroyed. Most all of these myths conclude that we are in the fourth world now... faced with destruction and re-creation because people are not learning to live in peace and harmony with each other and with the Earth. What is a myth anyway, I wondered? Western scholars have termed Native American stories and oral history as mythology - mythology being considered to be some fanciful, fairy tale idea that has no basis or grounding in reality. On the contrary, Native American myths are potent spiritual and historical accounts about the mankind's past, about the particulars tribe's experience of the world and about the plight of the human soul. Woven into these myths are many beliefs and spiritual ideas of the interrelationship of all things - animal, Earth and mineral, human and the divine or universal. The basic and most pervasive philosophy in all Native American creation myths is that human beings are passing through worlds of experience and changes in consciousness on a path of spiritual development. Human beings are learning to overcome selfishness, greed and disharmony.

One of the Dine or Navajo creation myths speaks of this process very clearly and profoundly:

In the beginning there appeared Begochiddy who was the child of the sun (creator) and who was both man and woman with blue eyes and golden hair. This being was responsible for all Earth children. In the first world, Begochiddy created all things for the first beings on Earth. But, after awhile, the first beings were not happy. Begochiddy then planted a big reed which grew higher and higher up into the second world. Here Begochiddy created many, many more things and the world (perhaps consciousness) was expanded with clouds, more color and more plants and animals. Things were good for awhile but eventually the second world human beings became discontent. Begochiddy decided to destroy the second world and try again. He led some of the people up into the third world. The third world was extremely beautiful and full of wonder and magic. People lived in harmony for a long time and many cultures came about and flourished all around the world. But men and women began to quarrel with each other and eventually such disharmony came about that Begochiddy destroyed the world with water. Some people barely survived and were led to the fourth (present) world. The fourth world was rich and fertile and the people were given many different types of seeds and sent out in all directions to create their lives and to create their own worlds. But Begochiddy gave all the people a stern warning: The fourth world would be destined for destruction just like the previous worlds if the people did not live in harmony and respect for each other and nature.

What amazed me about the Navajo creation story that was going through my mind was that in each world human beings were developing towards more creative freedom themselves. Begochiddy is represented as the male-female creator who leads human beings on a path of physical, mental and spiritual growth so that they might take some responsibility in the universal drama of creation. Begochiddy was caught in a process of creation and re-creation trying to perfect both the world and the beings which inhabited it. Is this not the reflection of all universal creation? Is it not destruction versus creation over and over until some ultimate divine level of existence is reached? Is this not the path of the human soul-to be born, to live, to die and be reborn to live again on its path toward spiritual perfection? Is this not the path for societies, cultures and all humanity - to be born, to live, to die and be reborn again in order to achieve harmony, peace, brother - and sisterhood?

It was good to get back home. Jessie and the boys had been worried. I was glad to see them safe, warm and happy. Later that night, after a wonderful meal and warm evening with my family, I dreamed about another totem...

CHAPTER XI

R ISING FROM THE VALLEY FLOOR, the Sangre de Cristo mountains towered over every horizon and sparkled like giant crystals in an ecliptic sun. It was March 20th, 1991, the spring equinox. Like so many times before, the scarlet dawn this morning pene-trated my consciousness and caused me to reflect upon the mystical happenings of my past and to accept a new creative impulse and purpose into my life: I needed to find another pine log to begin sculpting. I had been having another recurring dream in which I was creating a strong and ancient-looking totem.

A high degree of spiritual energy exists in the valley of Amalia. One needs only to be open to receive it. Jessie, the boys and I were very open and strong receivers when we arrived in Amalia probably because we had lived a relatively peaceful, healthy and healing life in the wooded hills of Maine. Over the past three or four months, though, we all had experienced vivid dreams and unconscious awakenings which had forced us to confront our fears and insecurities. Even the boys had grown amazingly in many ways... especially Jonathon. It was as if he had been confronting some terrible beast from the deep unconscious realms or from a past life experience - working through some overwhelming fears early in his life rather than later. I knew that his soul would be further advanced as he reached adulthood than the souls of many people who never work through their deepest fears until late in their lives.

I had long before realized that my children had been sent to me for an important purpose of growth and development. They, in turn, were helping me with my growth and development. This is true of all parent-child relationships and the Great Grandfather-Grandmother Creator had revealed to me that conception between a man and a woman in this day and age does not involve the creation of a new soul. Conception in these end times is a process by which souls come together for short interludes and learning experiences here on Earth by choice or by higher direction. All souls that exist on Earth today were long ago created during more tropical or 'divine' times. The population explosion on Earth today is the "rising up of all souls", so to speak, before the final resurrection. Every soul that has ever existed here in this solar system is being given a chance to balance out his or her spiritual growth. All the terrible afflictions and problems that individuals and societies face today are only catalysts for this growth.

The sun's rays were now warming my chilled body and I wondered about the age of my own soul. I knew that I had lived many times before and I had vivid memories about my past life in Atlantis and the third world, thanks to the mystical experience of 1977 during my long fast. I wondered how old I really was. Had I or any other souls lived on Mars or Chiron long ago before the planet Earth had cooled enough for the material bodies of human beings? Could it be that there was a direct link to the planet Mars in the history of human culture? While in Taos two weeks earlier, I had bought a cassette tape of what I thought would be some interesting music. I had never heard this particular music and was drawn to the tape by the title: *The Monuments of Mars*. When I opened the tape to play it later that same day, I was shocked to find a photograph of the Cydonian region of Mars which has many pyramids protruding from the sand. The photograph was no hoax. It was a computer enhanced version of a photo produced by

NASA from the 1976 Martian probe. I had sat down that very night and had written to the address provided in the outer jacket for more information about the ruins on Mars and had received the material just three days before. Some strange doorway between my conscious and unconscious mind had opened up it seemed for my dreams in recent weeks had been of an ancient place unlike any place on Earth that I knew about. The dreams were of a barren world and of a culture far advanced but in a state of quiet desperation. I was an artist and sculptor in that world, intensely involved in my work of creating giant stone sculptures. What I remember most vividly about the dreams is the lack of any familiar sculpting tools. All I had was a large crystal by which I would project my creative vision towards the stone. It was as if the atoms of the stone would be magically re-arranged according to my mental images.

There were other things about these dreams that I remembered vividly. All the people around me were anxious and seemed to be waiting for something. I remember looking up towards the sky along with the other people towards a very brilliant blue-green star. Many people had gone to that star already to escape the rapidly changing environmental conditions on their own planet. Upon waking from the dreams, I knew that the blue-green star was Earth and I was now coming to realize that the planet I was on in the dreams was Mars. It makes sense, I thought… that human beings once lived on the planet Mars. After all, Mars is a terrestrial planet much like Earth and Venus. Mars is farther from the sun and, naturally, would cool faster, thus losing its ability to support material life as we know it. Earth is the middle planet and, like Mars, is cooling off slowly. Earth too would someday lose its ability so support human life. Mankind was not helping the matter either. Destruction of the Earth's biosphere was accelerating this process. Venus, on the other hand, is still hot and virgin. Someday Venus could become a very fertile, lush garden much like the Earth was many, many ages ago.

I wondered about the ruins on Mars. According to the photos and information that I now had, these pyramids and other stone structures were identical to the pyramids and structures here on Earth and in some cases, were even more advanced. There were pyramids like the ones in Egypt and the ones in Central America. There was even the image of a sphinx which had a sort of inverted connection to the sphinx in Egypt. This was a very far-reaching and powerful discovery. Why wasn't this knowledge becoming well known among people in America? I would find out later that the United States Government was racing to cover up and discredit this information as fast as they could. For what reasons though... God only knows.

The boys and I hooked up the trailer to the truck around noon time and headed for a sawmill in Questa, 20 miles away. While driving by a week earlier, I had noticed a whole yard full of seasoned pine and spruce logs. I was hoping to purchase one and get it lifted into the trailer cradle. While we drove, I thought about what the Hopi Elders had said about the total eclipse that would occur that summer on July 11th. Somehow, this eclipse was very important. At least it was for me. I wanted to know more about eclipses and about this eclipse in particular. Having had a strong interest in astronomy and astrology over the years, I knew that I would easily be able to do some research about the subject over the next few days. For now though, I turned my concentration back to the wood-yard in Questa. The boys and I had arrived and were looking over the huge western pine and spruce logs. The owner of the yard was a curious man who turned out to be very interested in wood sculptures. He had been saving all kinds of stumps, twisted logs and odd wood pieces for years thinking that he might find someone to free the animals and objects that he saw in them. We talked for nearly an hour before I decided that I needed to pick out a log and get it loaded. He was very helpful and soon we were heading back for Amalia with a 25 foot perfectly straight spruce log safely secured in the trailer cradle.

Later that evening in my astrological books, I found some information on eclipses and the eclipse cycles of this century. I learned that there are always at least two solar eclipses a year and, in some years, there can be four or five. By far though, most these eclipses are not total eclipses but partial or annular. Total eclipses that last for up to seven minutes are very rare and they are the most significant eclipses. There had already been two of these rare eclipses this century: one in 1955 and one in 1973. The third one would occur this coming summer on July 11th, 1991. This was a very unusual astronomical occurrence. In the past three thousand years, there had only been 35 of these rare seven minute total eclipses and three of them would shadow the 20th century. All three of these rare eclipses have or will occur in the constellation of Gemini. According to all the ancient astrological meanings given to this constellation, Gemini rules all aspects of communication. The Gemini god is Mercury which has always been associated with "Winged Messenger". This is not surprising if one considers the explosion in all forms of communication technology that has characterized this century. Human beings have even developed *winged* travel in the past one hundred years. This too, is not surprising, considering that Gemini also rules forms of travel. And there have been tremendous new uses of communication technology even within our travel machines, such as computers in the dashboards of automobiles and planes.

The sign Gemini has been traditionally associated with the air we breath: the oxygen that gives us life. Mankind has drastically altered the balance of oxygen in the atmosphere. All of the aspects of life attributed to the sign Gemini throughout the ages have been 'eclipsed' by great change. As I sat and digested the above information, my mind was already synthesizing other bits of knowledge together with these new realizations. All of the modern communication technology has been made possible only through the discovery and use of quartz crystals. Scientists are able to grow artificial crystals in laboratories which facilitated the mass production of silicon chips which now are in virtually everything we use today. We are living in a crystal technology. We have realized the power of crystals and applied these realizations to the material world. I could only imagine what possibilities lie ahead for humanity if we ever begin to apply the power of crystals toward the spiritual realms. I knew from past research, and now from dreams, that modern human beings are not the first to use crystals. Perhaps today's discoveries in crystal technology are only rediscoveries or unconscious memories of ancient knowledge.

The legendary meanings of eclipses is most revealing. Usually one specific area of the Earth's surface experiences a direct total eclipse overhead every three or four centuries. On average, every place on Earth will experience a total eclipse within a 450 year period. It can happen, though, that one area could experience two total eclipses (not the rare 7 min. eclipses) within a few-year period or none for two-thousand years, as the eclipse cycles are very complicated and actually evolve according to the stability of all the planetary movements within this solar system and the movements of the galaxy. It has long been believed by many cultures, especially by the more astronomically advanced ones, that a major total eclipse would activate the deep unconscious and inner sacred energies of both nature and human beings. Both new levels of consciousness and past realms of consciousness could be energized, depending on the needs of the Earth and its living beings in the specific area that the eclipse would take place. The ancient astronomers and mystics carefully plotted eclipse cycles because they realized how they foretold change in all the realms of material and human existence.

The eclipse coming this summer was expected to last nearly seven minutes and be directly overhead Mexico City and many sacred Mayan - Toltec temple sites. At the peak of the eclipse, the axis of the shadow would reach closer to the center of the Earth than any of the total eclipses of the 20th and 21st century. Perhaps many people would experience an unconscious awakening that, in some way, would directly relate to the ancient Mayan and Toltec cultures. I knew that I was beginning to experience a strong unconscious flow of dreams and the mystical flow of conscious events in my life were making me aware of the nature and origin of Central American culture. My journey to the Hopi people, who were descendants of·the Central American cultures, had evidently been the doorway to the much deeper purpose of my calling. In recent weeks, I had dreamed about carving Toltec statues of a "Divine Human Being" which still exist and are standing among the ruins of Tula, Mexico. It would not be until later that summer, during the height of this special eclipse in July, that I would come to understand what was really going on in my life. I had been born under the constellation of Gemini just before the first of the three major eclipses in May, 1955. I knew from my research that total eclipses usually come hand-in-hand with great periods of change. My life thus far had been one change after another. The most profound change of all though was happening within my deepest mind. Could it be that my life had been somewhat pre-destined to a high degree? It was a scary thought but, as I had done so many times in recent years, I accepted the changes in all aspects of my life and went forward following my now strengthened inner guidance.

CHAPTER XII

EARLY APRIL BROUGHT SOME MAJOR CHANGES to the lives of Jessie, the boys and me. The boys' natural mother had been calling more frequently from Maine to express her feelings about being so far away from her sons. Jason and Jonathon were missing their mother and, at the same time, Jessie was feeling a little burned-out with her role as a stepmother. I had never been the type of father that was revengeful or possessive in terms of the children spending time with their mother. I had only been there when their mother had not. Early in the boy's lives she had turned away from responsible motherhood and gone down a path of self-abuse. Her relationships with men were characterized by use and abuse as she went from one alcoholic to another. Her father had been a terribly abusive alcoholic. I think that she was looking to heal her relationship with him through other men even though he had drunk himself to death... literally. Our relationship had not worked out because I was not abusive and she couldn't heal all the hurt and anger through me. It had been hard for me to let go of the whole situation. I had bailed her out of one financial mess after another and tried to be a friend, which often created a lot of tension with my second wife, Jessie. Jessie was an alcoholic and I guess I had just gone from one care-taking situation to another, although she was a responsible person despite her addictions. Both the boys' mother and Jessie played an extremely important role in my own emotional growth as I needed to realize that I could not heal my own abusive mother through my relationships with women. I needed to let go of the past.

Now it seemed I was against the wall. Jessie needed the space to go on in her life and face her own problems without continuing to escape through taking care of the children and me. The boys' mother was pleading with me to trust her and let the children come live with her. Her mother, the boys' grandmother, was also calling with promises of moral support and indicating that she would watch out for the children if they could come back to Maine for awhile. While fishing one sunny afternoon in the Rio Costilla, the boys and I talked about it. Although they were very young, I could sense their need to experience life with their mother and I knew that she needed to experience the joys and responsibilities of motherhood. I could not be the one to hold them back. It was a very hard decision for me – probably the most difficult decision of my life. I needed time alone to think about it all. I could feel the force of change pulling at my heart and soul and it was not a good feeling.

It was one of those warm mornings in early April that I hiked up into the mountains behind the house in order to find the answers I needed. The icy chill of winter was still gripping the arroyos that were hidden from the path of the sun. But the contrast of the cold in the these places to the warmth of the southern exposed hillsides was very conducive to solving my inner conflict about what path I should take with the boys. On the one hand, I remembered how cold and insensitive their mother had been at times and how she had caused so much pain and emotional turmoil for the boys. On the other hand, I knew that the love and support I had given them thus far would help to keep them feeling secure and safe through any potential difficulty. We were very close and I knew that no distance, however long, could block out the communication of our hearts. I would have to put my trust in the Divine and let them go. Perhaps she had changed and, if she had not, the boys needed to know the reality of their mother even at their young age. I decided that I would give it a trial test for one year and try to keep a close watch on their situation when they returned to Maine. What else could I do? I could never stand in the way of a natural life process even if it meant losing my sons for awhile. Maybe I needed some time, too. I felt guilty for having such a thought but yet I couldn't completely suppress that possibility. As I started back, I was in peace. I'm always all right with things once I take the time to work them out in my heart...

I was following a wide arroyo down the mountain side, looking at the layers of fresh Earth and geological past recently left exposed by the melting of the winter snow up on higher terrain. Huge chunks of quartz were everywhere. I had never seen such a high concentration of crystal-silicon based material. I scooped up a handful of the loose soil and could see that it was nothing but quartz; right down to the tiniest particle. Every step that I took in that arroyo seemed to connect my mind deeper and deeper to my innermost being. It was a connection to my sacred self - the altar of my soul.

Suddenly, it was there: the one thing that would change many aspects of my life and perception of the world forever. I had followed the arroyo around a sharp bend and came face to face with a large cluster of clear crystals, all grown together like the petals of a giant lotus flower. It was beautiful! In the middle of the cluster was a very large and thick crystal with a well-defined and widened point. All of the other crystals seemed to grow around this one specific crystal like children or serious students of eternal perfection. I could not take my eyes off that crystal. I wanted to hold it. I knew that I could not leave that place without it. I felt so much strength, wisdom and power emanating from its beautiful form. There was a bonding going on between my being and that crystal which I felt helpless to stop. How would I free it from the huge cluster? The cluster was only partially exposed with tons of quartz above it. I had no tools to chip it out. I could come back, I thought, but yet I could not bring myself to leave. Anxiously, I reached out to touch it. It was like touching a raw nerve of the Earth itself as I could feel its connection to the planet's fields of energy. Then, as if in a magical dream, the crystal broke free and fell into my hand. I couldn't believe it. I stood in shock for what seemed to be an eternity just looking deep within the magical stone. It was very old and had millenniums of secrets about creation frozen inside of its many prisms. I could see deep within these secrets for a moment. It was a seeing that my two physical eyes could not be a part of - only the third eye could see in this realm.

I had a strange feeling in the center of my forehead as I put the crystal inside of my coat pocket holding it tightly in my hand. All of a sudden a flood of memories overtook my thoughts. I had experienced this feeling in the center of my forehead years before. It happened at the mushroom site near the University of Maine. I remember one night in particular when I had partaken in a delicious meal of nut flavored mushrooms after a long day on campus. After the meal, I laid down on a carpet of pine needles in total rapture with the forest surrounding me like a giant living tapestry. It was during times such as these that my consciousness would merge with the very fabric of life itself. This one night in particular I had drifted into a semi-conscious state when I felt a curious ache between my eyes in my lower forehead. When I reached to touch the spot where the ache was coming from, I felt a tender area rather like a soft mushy hole. I tried to focus on the spot in my mind to understand what I was feeling and could see many little tiny mushrooms growing right out of my forehead.

Over the years, I have come to realize that those tiny mushrooms growing in the center of my forehead represented an awakening of a different type of 'seeing' and a more intuitive level of awareness. But it had been only an awakening. My life from that point on would be a constant challenge to develop this intuitive vision or third eye. Sometimes many months or even years have gone by without any noticeable development of this ability, but it never goes away. It waits for its own time, and one just picks up where one leaves off in the intuitive growth process, no matter how stormy or difficult the physical and emotional passages of life may be. Mushrooms have always been associated with the magical and hidden sides of life. They grow at night under the stars and in the light of the moon. They feed on the decaying remains of the conscious-daytime world, although some mushrooms appear not to be feeding on any Earthly matter whatsoever. There are certain mushrooms that cannot be artificially grown in dark labs. The ancients believed that these mushrooms were the flesh of the gods magically seeded during the midnight hours. Many native cultures have used certain mushrooms to experience and communicate with the Divine. They never used them as an escape or for thrills. I was never aware of eating any magical mushrooms but I evidently must have. Now I was on a path of increasing mystical awareness. I don't think I could have walked a different path even if I had wanted to.

Traditionally, throughout the ages, there have been two opposing ways of "seeing" the world. Seeing, in the material sense, with our two physical eyes is the most basic. From this type of seeing have come all

natural sciences and the "rational mind". Seeing through
the third, intuitive eye, on the other hand, is the basis
of all mysticism and spiritual understanding. Ever since
the early Greek philosophers perfected their systems of
rational conception which attempted to separate human
beings from nature and the divine creative force,Western
culture has marched through time condemning and
destroying individuals and cultures that valued spiritual
and mystical intuition higher than reason. This incredible
drive to "know" everything, to classify and control
everything, has only left the basic beauty of the world
pilfered and nearly destroyed. Native American cultures
knew the dangers of human reason unchecked and
unbalanced with intuitive understanding. They were not,
as some people have believed, primitive cultures that
had never 'advanced' enough in their mental evolution
to develop and value the rational mind above all other
human abilities.

To the contrary, my research and experience of
Native American cultures had proved a different path
of cultural development altogether. Native Americans
had already advanced beyond the idea and realm of the
rational individual as being separate from nature. More
and more historical and archeological evidence confirms
that many Native American cultures were actually migra-
ting away from corrupt centers of civilization in Central
America, China, Europe, "Atlantis" and other places. The
creation myths of both the Hopi and Navajo that I had
recently encountered tell of these corrupt worlds of the
past. The whole social design and codes of behavior of
Native cultures were often full of safeguards against
selfish individualism and greed. It was better to be in the
world totally connected than to be in the world with
conceptions of being separate and/or above nature. For
God's sake, I thought, what was wrong with giving

thanks to the sun, the rain, the wind and the stars with magical ceremonies and beautiful creations of art? What was wrong with being thankful for the things used and borrowed from nature? What was wrong with respecting every living thing - be it another person, a spirit, an animal or a piece of cedar bark?

It was interesting, too, I thought, that the rational aspects of being have always been associated with men more so than with women and the intuitive aspects of being associated with women more than with men. Therefore, societies controlled by men up to the present have been highly rational, controlling and very separate from nature. These societies create strong egotistical individuals that gravitate towards greed and selfishness. Native Americans were very aware of this inner nature of the male aspect of being. They had strong checks and balances to control this. In many tribes, men were not allowed to own or control the material things by which the society subsisted. Women distributed the food, hides and all the material things. They also managed and 'owned' the shelters. Even today, this practice continues on some Western reservations like the Hopi.

Native Americans valued the form of *seeing* that comes about in anyone who stops long enough to become peacefully still and understand that all things in this world are interrelated completely. Human beings are in the world and of the world connected to even the most desolate piece of rock in the most desolate place on Earth, for just about every element that exists on this planet exists within our bodies and minds. The consciousness of the *connectedness of all things* is the most liberating experience of freedom that humans are capable of experiencing. With this consciousness, one has no need for fences, property lines, banks and the like because simple levels of respect would suffice. This is exactly what the Europeans encountered when they came to this continent. There were hundreds and hundreds of individual tribes sharing this great land from the Arctic to the Antarctic. There were no prisons. There were no mental institutions. And there were no great tracks of land raped and spoiled for generations to follow.

Native cultures from the Americas to New Zealand understood the connected nature of human beings to the elements of the Earth. They understood the magical and special qualities of crystals long ago. Crystals were somehow connected to the whole global consciousness of the planet and were directly linked to the development of human consciousness. After all, I thought, what do crystals actually do? What is the nature of crystals and why are they related to consciousness at all? The fact is they somehow and in some way receive, store and transmit energy - electrical information. This is exactly what the human brain does! It would be easy to follow from this line of thought that crystals are somehow conscious on a level that closely relates to human consciousness. This was a very interesting realization for me as I finally reached the valley floor of Amalia and the line of cottonwood trees which surrounded the house my family and I were renting.

CHAPTER XIII

B Y MID-APRIl, the ground under the totem trailer was covered with wood chips and sawdust. I had been carving the white spruce log furiously for two or three days ever since Jessie and I had returned from the airport in Albuquerque. It had been very painful to let the boys go even though I knew that it was the right thing to do. I think the emotional energy created by the whole situation provided a stronger intensity in my work on the new totem. I wondered too, if the crystal that I had found in the arroyo was also generating strong levels of creative energy. Every morning, before I started cutting and shaping the Toltec image, I placed the crystal on the trailer near me feeling that it was somehow connecting me to some ancient realm. As the days went by, turning longer and warmer, I merged for hours at a time with the Toltec statue that was unfolding before me. The whole creative process this time seemed so strangely magical. There was not the stress and strain of shaping the wood that I had experienced on the Hopi totem. It seemed as though the statue was already in the log and that I was just removing all the excess wood like rusted layers of time. There was no doubt that I was opening up to some deep reality within my soul or unconscious mind. Every line and every curve of the Toltec was familiar. Each aspect of the process had meaning for me and each part of the finished Toltec revealed ancient knowledge and spiritual understanding about human existence on Earth.

From the bottom of the log came the shape of two ancient feet emerging from the head (the mind) of a dreaming god-being of Toltec or Mayan character. From this point upwards on the log, a fifteen-foot tall Toltec human image began to appear. But this was no ordinary human being coming out of the wood before me. In every aspect, this being was of Divine nature: illuminated and endowed with spiritual power. It seemed that the dreaming form on the bottom was creating this perfected being with its crystal pure mental energy. I had intuitive flashes that many successions of beings and acts of creation would continue all the way down the rest of the log and into its roots had that part been there. It did not matter if it was there ultimately. I could sense the time and history of that tree and its biological-genetic past. Just as the tree was the product of countless cycles of form and formlessness, so too were human beings and their dreams.

It was a strange feeling to stand there next to that log and sense the deeper reality of its whole essence and it was even stranger to have the same feelings about the Toltec image. Could it be that I was sensing the deeper reality of human existence? Somewhere, in some past realm, there was more to this totem than I could have ever imagined. There was information and meaningful truth about the creation of human beings. Only the most illumined soul could ever grasp it all. I knew that I could never meet the task but I had a pretty good idea that I would spend the rest of my life attempting to grasp as much as I could about the purpose of human beings here on Earth and about our relationship to the Divine centers of universal creation. I also knew that the key to understanding mankind's future was in these long ago forgotten mysteries which this Toltec statue represented. Somehow too, this totem was a part of me. It was coming out of my own being and unconscious connection to the collective unconscious mind of humanity. I felt an overwhelming need to be careful and gentle with the transforming wood for the Toltec image seemed almost alive at times and, if I cut too deep, I may have actually wounded it. I know it was a crazy feeling when looking back because, in actuality, it was just a piece of wood. But it was not crazy when I was working on it.

The whole creative process happening on that trailer in the valley of Amalia by early May was alive. Even the wood was alive for me. The soft, wet fiber exposed after removing each outer layer felt like the flesh of an immortal person. In a way I guess, it was. All of the elements in the tree had come together out of a long cycle of continuous death and rebirth over and over for thousands of years. Every fiber in that log had elements of once living things and even of human beings. How many atoms, I wondered, were there in the sap and water of that tree that once flowed through the bodies of ancient plants, animals and humans. Water is the binding spirit of life and is the one substance that flows through time and all forms of life continuously without much elemental change. The water in my own body comes and goes constantly within this whole natural process and is, in part, what keeps me alive. The rains bring water from other parts of the world and I end up with elements of water that once flowed through tropical trees, arctic oceans and human beings from other cultures. This is one aspect of the connectedness of all things.

So many transforming realizations and intuitive flashes passed through my mind during the many long hours that I worked on the Toltec sculpture. I remember wondering if the crystal was actually responsible for the increase in creative energy and spiritual insight that I was experiencing. There was one morning that I decided to leave the crystal put away inside the house. Whether it was my imagination or not, I don't know, but I almost ruined the part of the totem that I was working on at the time. I quickly realized that, illusion or not, the crystal was facilitating the creation of the Toltec!

There was something about those mountains also.

The Sangre de Cristos extend from Colorado down through New Mexico and link up with the Sierra Madres in Mexico. The whole great mountain chain that surrounds Amalia continues down towards Central America right into ancient Mayan and Toltec country. All my life, I had connected, in a mystical way, with the spirit of the Earth of wherever I traveled and perhaps I was connecting with the Toltec spirits by just being in those mountains. What was driving me to create such an unusual thing? What was my life coming to these days anyway? Everything in my life had changed or was changing dramatically and it seemed, sometimes, that I was not in control of my own immediate future. By day I sculpted on the Toltec with a feverish intensity. By night I painted and made moose and deer hide medicine bags. The creative levels within my soul bordered on really being out of control. Jessie felt like I was pushing her out of my life even though we both knew our paths were separating. My interest in Native American art and culture was increasing but not on super-ficial levels. My connection to Native American spirituality was coming from someplace within my being and from my distant past.

I do know that there were many Native American cultures all down through those mountains and I was very drawn to them. Before my children were born, I had traveled one winter into Central Mexico and lived in a mountain town called Zapotecas. At that time, I was committed never to return to the United States again. I had gotten totally frustrated with the selfish, material culture of my country and wanted out. I was searching for myself and was very young and emotionally im-mature. The social conditions among the Spanish were not much better than America as there was the same basic greedy aspirations in people and the Native Indians were treated like dirt. The Spanish treated the

Native Mayan people worse than the Anglos treated the Black and Native American people back in the United States. There was no way that I could be a part of the Spanish culture and I came very close to disappearing into the Mayan culture of the area but, at the last minute, I realized that I had unfulfilled responsibilities and spiritual growth still waiting for me back in Maine. I was not ready for the path I was heading down. I was not free from inherited personal, family and social karma.

I had been running too - running, away from my emotions and from a painful relationship. Shortly before leaving for Zapotecas, I had been involved with an older woman in Central Maine. Every time we made love we talked about creating a little girl. I was ready for children at the time and ready to experience the full and total act of procreation. The idea of creating children made the whole sexual experience more profound and complete. This all happened about the time I was building my first home - the log cabin where I had the first totem dream. This woman came to me one hot July afternoon while I was peeling and shaping logs for the cabin walls. "By the way," she said, "I had an abortion today. Will you pay for half the costs?" Well, I pretty near lost my mind for awhile. I had not even known she was pregnant and I couldn't believe that everything we talked about during our shared summer nights had come to mean absolutely nothing to her. She was angry with men and this was just another way for her to work out her deep levels of anger. I was not the real issue nor was our baby. It seemed to me that she was still clinging to the past, unable to let go of the emotional harm inflicted upon her by other men. In any case, I took it very hard. Thus, my trip to Central Mexico was nothing other than an attempt to escape emotional pain and growth. I was hurt and I was vulnerable. There was no way I would have survived potential difficulties and struggles in the Zapotecas Mountains without first coming back to face my emotional fears and insecurities.

While in Zapotecas, I had a very powerful dream that I'll never forget. It was a dream that ended up freeing me from the pain, hurt and anger from all the experience of abuse in my childhood - from my mother and from all the distraught relationships of my young adulthood. (I had never confronted my mother or any women with whom I had been involved with up to that point in my life. I always just ran away) But, in the dream, I was trapped in a room with my mother and these particular women. They were all coming towards me, yelling, demanding my soul. Finally, a dam broke inside of me. With an intensity that burned every cell in my body, I screamed loud enough to break a large plate glass window out of the wall. I let it all out in a rush of feeling and emotion that felt like a hurricane wind. Then, all of the sudden, my soul was about 1,000 pounds lighter and my body lifted up and very peacefully floated out of the broken window. I did not have to run anymore and began the journey home to New England the day after. The journey was not an easy one, for most of my money had gone to the needs of small children in Zapotecas plaza.

I never have believed that I was a victim of life at any time. I always have had an intuitive sense that I was only experiencing the things that I needed to experience in order to find a spiritual balance in this lifetime. In past lives, I may have made bad emotional decisions or have been heartless and uncaring at some point in the history of my soul. Thus, all of the emotional experience that was a part of my journey here on Earth was meant to help me awaken, heal and grow. Now here I was again at another emotional crossroad with my second wife, Jessie. Our paths were parting. She knew it and I knew it. There was part of me that wanted to hold on to Jessie for fear of being alone and I think she went through the same last minute panic. By early May though, she had left to stay with some friends in Taos and I was making plans to stay for awhile in Santa Fe. Most people would probably not understand how a person could love someone so much and yet let them go so easily. This was exactly the case with Jessie and me. I loved her more than any woman I had known but knew in my heart that she was lost in my strengths, spirituality, and creativity. Her own spirituality was undeveloped and yearning to be explored. I opened up so much for her - so many doors to realms she never knew existed. I did these things not intentionally, but by being myself and not being afraid to follow my dreams.

As I packed for Santa Fe, I was still putting the finishing touches on the Toltec statue, helping a friend build a small mountain cabin on the Rio Costilla, and sculpting an eight-foot high grizzly bear to stand in front of the local general store. There was an uncanny purpose for that great grizzly sculpture being at that particular place as well as for why I sculpted it at all. Directly across the valley loomed the mountain canyon that Jessie, the boys and I had climbed up into the day before I collapsed with fever. The grizzly bear was tall and strong with his teeth blazing towards the heart of the canyon. He was standing there despite all possible adversity as if to prove his courage and fearlessness. That bear was me and that canyon was the unknown. I would come back to Amalia someday. I would come back to give thanks for the many blessings of personal fortitude that this incredible mountain valley brought Jessie, the children and myself. The last of the winter ice was gone... gone with the rush of the Rio Costilla heading for the Gulf of Mexico.

CHAPTER XIV

A FTER LEAVING AMALIA, I STOPPED IN TAOS to visit Jessie. We decided to spend a week or two together before starting on our separate paths, and planned to travel west into Arizona. I wanted to try selling the new totem in Flagstaff or Sedona and I wanted to show Jessie more of the west. I knew that it would be good for her. Vast expanses of desert and mountains are good for the human soul. The panoramic beauty and endless horizons cause one to come out of secure inner worlds for awhile and to let go of petty worries. So many people were coming to New Mexico and Arizona these days to experience that openness. There are a great many sacred places in the southwest - places where only ageless time dwells. People come and create little islands of community here and there but the vast expanses of land never cease to exist.

While Jessie put her things together for the trip, I laid down on the truck tailgate facing the totem trailer. Glistening in the hot Taos sun before me was the giant Toltec statue fully completed and freshly layered with fiberglass resin. Earth tones of rust, tan and brown were fused with scarlet red, bright yellow and glowing orange. In all, it was twenty feet tall and had a beautiful golden eagle on top. With a twelve foot wing span, the eagle stood balanced on a blazing yellow sun which was rising out of a head-dress or crown atop the Toltec being. Many sacred symbols adorned the statue in special places. On the head-dress there were images of pyramids from long ago symbolizing ancient knowledge and wisdom. On the chest was a sacred symbol of love, protection and eternal life. In the middle or groin section of the Toltec was a brown and scarlet red shield which also was covered with sacred symbols. This was the most interesting part of the totem, for there was a powerful message for me here. The shield protected the emotional and sexual center of the Toltec and the symbols profoundly spoke to the place of my inner knowing.

Human beings, by far, have the most advanced sexual centers in all the universe in terms of material existence. Souls from all over the realms of creation come here to this planet just to experience this procreative power in the flesh and blood. In the beginning, when both the male and female aspects of our Creator emerged in this world, sexual experience was a very sacred thing. Our Creator wanted it to be this way. The sacred act of sex was meant to be the re-union of the male and female aspects of Divine being. Through this union comes the miracle of creation and through this union comes the experience of cosmic energy: the same energy that is the very nature of our Creator, God. Yes, every time a man and a woman come together in physical union and in love, the doorway to the Divine realms opens up for a moment allowing the wondrous experience of original creation when our Creator implanted its power and being into the material world. This feeling is an ultimate feeling for sure. The experience of it is one of the driving forces of the human condition. To pervert it is the beginning of self-destruction.

But, in this Toltec being, I saw something more. I saw that the shield also represented a very highly evolved emotional center. This being was both male and female. It had stood the test of countless life times on Earth. It had created new life over and over and had learned to master the responsibility and the love that was a part of it all. Eventually, this being realized its Godhood: its sacred connection to the original creation and to all eternity. It realized its male and female aspects and then united them in perfect balance. Now the shield protected these evolved centers of being so that there would not be a return to the divided and more difficult realms as can happen while still in the material world.

It is true that, once in while, in the history of humanity, certain individuals have emerged who had found this union between the male and female power. Every single culture has had one or more spiritual leaders that displayed the Divine nature that is potential for all. Many cultures found this balance within their societies. Most of the Native American cultures lived with a beautiful and almost Divine balance of the male and female. Only now, after almost total destruction of those Native cultures, are people finally realizing what was almost lost. All over this country and all over the world, a rapidly increasing interest in Native American spiritual beliefs was emerging. Perhaps, I thought, all was not destroyed or lost. Somehow, enough of their spiritual understandings had been kept whole and alive.

By late evening the following day, Jessie and I had arrived on Second Mesa. It was too late to visit Francisco and we were very tired. All day while driving, I had wondered about what I was told of Christ during my first visit here on Hopi land. I wondered if Christ truly was one of those individuals that had found Divine union and of how he had given so much love and hope to the Hopi people. He had done this during some of their most desperate times without making himself a king, priest, or some other worshiped authority. I thought about how he came to them, how he healed and fed them, how he helped them get on track spiritually and then just left quietly without any fanfare. Wasn't this just what he did in the Middle East? Truly this being of Christ was a Divine being.

The nights on the Hopi Mesas in early May are still bitter cold at times which made it hard for us to sleep. We had curled up together on the truck seat two or three hours earlier exhausted and tired but I found myself still awake thinking about all that I had learned about Christ since my drowning and spiritual contact with him. It had been hard for me to break through all the religious barriers in my attempt to really understand the core message of Christianity. So many perversions there were of a message so simple. My understandings came in part through serious study of theology and history, but mostly they came through fasting and mystical intuition. I thought about how the teachings of Christ interrelated with the beliefs of Native Americans.

Jesus Christ was born in spirit the day John the Baptist took him down to the river to be blessed with water. Water represented the spirit. To the Native American, water was one of the binding spirits of all life. From his baptism on, Christ taught of love for all people and for all things, as they are one. He revealed many truths about the nature of life and of the human soul. His examples of simplicity and humility were in sharp contrast to those of the Pharisees, Rabbis and other political-religious leaders of that time. He never taught any theological doctrines and he denounced the champions of hypocrisy because "they love the chief seats" and "bind heavy burdens, grievous to be born" with all sort of rules and regulations.

Christ emphasized humanity's beautiful and natural connection to the Divine and taught people how to get directly in touch with the spirit of God within their own hearts. Rules and regulations of every kind were by the convention of men for the purpose of the continued wealth and power of a few: "the letter killeth, but the spirit giveth life." This love spirit and emphasis on one's spiritual conduct in relation to the rest of the world was his central doctrine. Christ tried to show people that we are here to develop loving and peaceful relationships with all others including nature. This was exactly how the Native Americans lived. The ultimate concern that Christ had for humanity was for their spiritual awakening. Was this not the main concern for almost all of the great Native American leaders? For Christ, the true test of any person's character and the ultimate measure of a person's soul was by how they lived: by their deeds, by their works, and by their love for peace. It was not by how well they learned, interpreted and preached the legal doctrines of the day whether they be religious or political. But, of course, Christ was eventually put to death because of his teachings. The very culture, the very priests and rabbis that prophesied the first coming of Christ could not face the truths that he brought. They would let nothing challenge their *chief seats*.

In Native American culture, we find that the *seat of the chief* was a totally different thing altogether. The *chief* was not the ruler of others or the great holder of land and wealth. The chief was the person who had proved the highest levels of moral and spiritual character and one who always put love and peace first in the face of personal and social adversity. The chief was also the one who had the strength, wisdom and courage enough to bind the whole tribe together as one. The chief respected every person as equal and made sure that all the roles of tribal responsibility were fulfilled. By far though, the most important function of the Native American chief was to promote spiritual growth in others through his own spiritual examples. He or she made sure that the spirit-keepers and spirit-healers of the tribe were fully supported, protected and honored. If ever there was a people that follow the true examples of living given to us by Christ, I thought, it surely would be the Native Americans. They never needed lengthy scriptures and religious-legal doctrines. They passed down their spiritual codes through living examples and through unbroken chains of spiritual ceremonies. They never needed massive cathedrals or political institutions to enforce their religions. Their "religions" survived because they were pure and natural... and they related directly to the eternal nature of the human soul. I knew now, in my heart, that a horrible crime had been committed on the American continent when these cultures were ravaged and nearly destroyed. In the days that were to follow, I would experience tremendous pain and anguish over this realization. My God, I thought, Native Americans welcomed the Europeans and even helped them survive those first few harsh years. They taught the Europeans about plants and trees around the settlements and introduced new foods to them. The same thing had happened in Central America. Natives there already knew about Christ and about his message of peace and love. They knew about his return someday. Even though some of the tribes had fallen into decadent times (like the Aztecs), they still welcomed the greedy barons that were bearing the cross and message of Christ. What a crazy hypocritical people those Europeans were: to hate, steal, rape and murder in the name of Christ. Did they ever take time to read the New Testament that they were carrying?

I was being awakened to the fact that Christ appeared in cultures all over the world. He appeared in the Middle East during the Hebrew-Roman times, but not exclusively, for I knew that he had appeared all over the American continent near or about the same time in history. The reason he appeared to the Hebrew-Roman culture was to warn them about the dangers of their growing religious-political doctrines that led people away from the true altar of the Divine within one's heart and soul. He implanted a message of love and peace in cultures that were full of envy, hate and jealousy. Isn't it strange, I thought, that so many of those people who truly followed the examples of Christ and who lived in his spiritual light, were condemned and put to death? These were highly intuitive women or men who had developed their female-mystical and intuitive sides. Never would such a spiritual seeker be condemned or put to death in a Native American culture. Christ appeared to the people in the Middle East in an attempt to avert the growing forces of selfish individualism and empty spiritual doctrines. He came in peace and never once talked of war or rebellion, but yet was ridiculed and tortured. Then, John the Baptist was beheaded, and his head was delivered to the leaders of the Roman empire which eventually became the institution of Christianity! Tell me, I wondered, who were the true Christians? Who and where were the lost tribes talked about in the New Testament? My body shook with chills. In my soul I knew the answer to these questions and I knew that I would someday have to bring this message to my fellow human beings.

At dawn, I was still awake in the front of the truck reading different parts of the New Testament. I was hoping to find some answers to my now deepest concerns for understanding the relationship of Christ to the Native American people. It was in Matthew V that I found these answers:

"Blessed are the meek, for they shall inherit the Earth."

CHAPTER XV

A STEADFAST HOT AND DRY WIND from the west was sweeping over the top of Third Mesa by the time Jessie and I arrived at Francisco's in the late morning. Stunned and surprised at the sight of another totem showing up in his yard, he greeted us warmly. After looking over the Toltec giant, he invited us in. Shades of worry and apprehension lay directly under his warm friendly greeting though, and, as we talked, the source of this worry became clear. Francisco had been the spokesman for some of the Hopi Elders over past months and had interpreted the meaning of the Prophecy Totem to the political Hopi people on First and Second Mesa after my departure in late winter. When they found out that it related directly to their own ancient prophesies, trouble had begun - trouble that went all the way back to BIA in Washington. The political forces of greed and cultural destruction were winning the battle for Hopi land and the traditional people were being pushed further and further into isolation and material compromise. The last thing that these political forces wanted was someone or something stirring up spiritual issues.

I could see that Francisco was emotionally drained from struggling with the powerful opposing forces in his society. Deep tidal currents of tradition were pulling at his soul while the lure of material security and *modernism* was laid out before him on a red carpet. Leaders like Francisco needed to be controlled and won over, according to the political leaders. Francisco and I were about the same age. I could sense his yet undeveloped, deep levels of wisdom. His intense struggles were a part of his spiritual training for the present time. Somehow, I could see beyond the present and into the future. I could see that Francisco was a *Chief* in training.

Francisco was concerned about the Prophecy Totem being in the place that it was on Second Mesa. I could sense through him that the political Hopi people feared it now and Francisco affirmed that it needed to be brought up to Third Mesa. Within an hour, he had gathered a group of Hopi men to help lift the totem onto the trailer and then unload it at his house. We had to reposition the Toltec first to fit both totems on the trailer and I was not sure if it would hold the combined weight. The transport went well and by mid-afternoon, the Prophecy Totem laid on a makeshift cradle in Francisco's back yard. Where it would come to rest permanently was still an unresolved issue but Francisco had taken a stand.

By now, I was really questioning again the purpose of the Prophecy Totem as well as my part in the whole drama. I had never liked politics at all and I was never one to cause political trouble. I was just a country boy at heart and a very creative soul. I believed in peace and harmony. I had never hit anyone in my whole life. I never had to. Peace was an inherent part of my nature. I had passing moments of guilt for Francisco's now more intense conflict with tribal forces, but I realized that Francisco's struggles with both the modern and traditional aspects of his culture had been coming to a focus long before I arrived on the scene with the totem.

Francisco, too, was a man of peace. He was walking the middle road trying to bring both the opposite realms of his culture together in whatever way he could. He could see that his people had to take the best of both realms to create a better future. I felt a deep respect and love for Francisco that day. This feeling has never faded and someday... someday I would help him with his tremendous burden for a great sense of brotherhood was developing between us.

The ride to Flagstaff was hot and dry. The fierce west wind kept trying to lift the wings of the Toltec eagle as the truck labored to keep speeds of 45 miles per hour against the shifting atmosphere. Beside me in the truck sat my friend and companion Jessie. I could see that she was changing within by the hour. I think that the events of that day and the incredibly vast horizons had helped to expand her consciousness outward from her very insecure center for the first time in a long while. I could see deeper into her inner beauty than ever before. I could see her Divine nature as woman and I could sense my own soul through her. I had grown through so much of my own hurt and pain in the relationship and it was the same for her. What we had brought to each other in this life and what we had helped each other heal through were not just present life issues. I could sense our connection back in time and history to other realms of human experience, realms of comfort and love as well as realms of pain. Pain is very much a part of life. To be human and to develop spiritually towards our own Godhood is to experience all of these realms. In the material world of flesh and blood, pain is the cross of being. To be really alive is to feel with the heart and soul. All happiness and ecstasy are born out of this cross of being. Would anyone ever really choose a destiny free from hurt and pain if they had the choice? If they did, from what source of experience would they grow and spiral upwards out of the material realm towards the center of Divine Creation... which must be where we are all headed sooner or later. Life on Earth is a continuous and relentless effort on the part of all living things to be born, grow, reach upward towards the warm sun, experience, share and die to be reborn again to the same. Human beings are unique in that they can attain freedom from the material realm through spiritual development.

Human existence really is a strange paradox, I thought. The poet Gibran expressed it best: "You know there is a meaning in this life which Death does not conceal. But how could humanity attain a knowledge which comes only when the soul is freed from Earthly ties?"

Arctic winds and ice sweep out from the poles of this planet to meet the warming currents of air that expand from the Equator... a constant interplay between the realms of life and the realms of death. I wondered if people realized just how delicate this balance of life is within the vast ocean of cosmic dust and electromagnetic forces. It's a precious balance. There is no eternity here in the material world. Everything is always changing and our time is limited. We must eventually grow through the material realm and transcend things like pain and hurt which is a part of being here. Eternity is only a hope for us. For if we fail, our fate may be like the black holes that astronomers are discovering all over the universe. They are places where matter is sucked back into the cycles of destruction and re-creation. It is the same for human souls. We can choose the spiritual path of eternity or we can choose the opposite path: destruction and re-creation. Harmony and love are the binding forces of eternity. Disharmony is the friend of nothingness and destruction. A wise person would never try to shelter himself nor herself from necessary pain. This is one of our biggest problems in American society today, I thought. So many people are looking for ways to avoid pain. It's no wonder that the country borders on spiritual bankruptcy.

Human life is the experience of a multitude of feelings, desires, hopes and emotions which we must harmonize. That is our most important purpose and our first and foremost task. Many prophecies speak of the paradox of being and of how this present age of physical-mental existence will come to a climactic new beginning in spiritual being. The forces of Eternity and destruction are coming to claim what is due them. I could see that human history is on the brink of a tremendous and sudden change like a great cosmic war. I thought it was very interesting to ponder ancient mythology and astrology at this point. It has long been said that Mars symbolizes the primal-physical aspects of being. Venus is always associated with the future and spiritual realms. Is it some chance coincidence that humanity now exists on Earth in the middle of these two planets and aspects of being? Venus is love... Mars is war. Venus is the future... Mars is the past. It seems that the Earth is the middle ground of being and that the mind is the meeting point of body and spirit. As we drove onward against the fiery, dry wind, my mind focused on the passing scenery.

The land around me, the deserts of North America, were evidence of past sudden climactic changes on this planet. The endless rock formations in the Southwest were made when the ocean left this part of the Earth's surface and when torrents of inland water rushed to keep up with the receding ocean waters. Directly north of me was the Grand Canyon. I imagined that billions of gallons of water must have rushed over that area daily for a long time to create such a vast and deep canyon. Could Earth changes like this come again? Maybe the Hopi people had a very good reason for settling atop the high desert mesas even if it meant difficult and steep climbs up and down to their farmland.

I wondered, too, about the planet Mars. By now, I was developing a very strong interest in Mars research projects and I had a strong feeling that the Toltec statue that was moving along in the drag-wind of the truck was related to the possibility of past human existence on Mars. The pyramidal ruins in the Cydonian region of Mars were absolute physical proof of some distant connection in the past between humanity and the red planet. Computer-enhanced photos from the 1976 probe were revealing a very complex and advanced city still very well preserved in the cold and dry atmosphere on Mars. The planet's dry river beds, sand dunes and wind-blasted mountains are strikingly the same as many desert areas here on Earth.

High in the Andes Mountains of South America, there are miles and miles of cold-dry plains that are almost identical in terrain and climate to the surface of Mars in the Cydonian region. And what has been found on those plains but many lines, markers, animal and human shapes that cannot be fully seen except from the air. It has been theorized that these shapes and lines, as seen from the air, once had a very important meaning. Could it be that these shapes and lines were created to help guide the mass transport of human beings to this planet from a dying Mars? Could it be that these markers actually pointed to different climate and cultural areas around the globe? Did they give direction to incoming craft? I knew that these questions about the high Andes plains were not new. Many researchers have pondered these same questions. It was the continuous succession of dreams I was having recently, though, that was opening my consciousness to these past realms of humanity. The dreams were exposing me to a deep level of mystical experience.

One of the books that I had with me on the trip laid next to me on the seat. It was about Mexico - past and present. One of the chapters talked about Mayan mythology, history and the story of Quetzalcoatl. I had already realized that Quetzalcoatl was the same being as Christ. The interesting thing about this story is the relationship of Quetzalcoatl to the planet Venus. The legend is that Quetzalcoatl was tricked into an intoxicated state and committed an immoral-sexual act. Quetzalcoatl was so ashamed of his deed that he told the Mayan people that he had to leave. He had spent many years with the Mayans trying to help them create a beautiful civilization based on love and peace but the people were not ready to enter the spiritual realms completely. It was said that he went to create a new world on the planet Venus. In Christianity, Christ is synonymous with love. In all traditional mythology and astrology, love is synonymous with Venus. Someday the Earth will be dry, frozen and barren just like Mars for the Earth is surely changing in this direction now. Where will the human soul go then? Venus would seem to be the likely answer. Who can say that Venus is not ready for us now? If we were in spirit form and not in bodies, we may not feel heat and cold the same as we do now. In actuality, Venus may be ripe and ready for the collective human soul in spirit. The intense heat and low pressure atmosphere on the surface of Venus may be exactly what the soul of humanity needs to cleanse and purify itself... not unlike a giant collective sweat lodge. I remembered that when I drowned off the coast of Southern California years earlier, I had experienced the realm of the spirit after I had departed from my body. There was no sense of heat or cold. There was just a beautiful feeling of being. It was a whole different realm altogether. In this realm, one may be able to visit any planet in the solar system. Without a physical body to hold us steadfast in the world of sense and emotion, who's to say where we could go and what we could experience?

Change is the basic element of being here in the

material world and change on very drastic levels has characterized human experience from the beginning. The surface of this planet is changing rapidly now. Oxygen regulating forests are disappearing, raging storms and earthquakes are increasing. The atmosphere has reached a critical stress point and so has the electro-magnetic and gravitational balance of the planet. The possibility of severe food shortages as the desert areas increase in size has already become a reality and I wondered how long the Earth's biosphere could support such a mass of "intelligent" bones and flesh. Many prophesies foretell the return of the gods to help humanity through this inevitable change. They talk about a new heaven and a new Earth. Some of the Native American prophecies point us to the planet Venus. Venus is hot and steamy now but the Earth was once the same and it's a strong possibility that spiritual beings exist on Venus already.

Changes of great magnitude have happened on the Earth more than once, I thought. The dinosaurs disappeared in a sudden catastrophic change and, down under the Antarctic sheets of ice, huge woolly mammoths have been found frozen while still standing with fresh tropical plants in their stomachs. Now that's a sudden climactic change for sure. I realized now that prophecies about sudden and catastrophic change on the surface of this planet in the near future were very realistic and I wondered just how these changes would render the collective human soul. Perhaps I would find the answer to this question someday soon as I searched for more understanding of both the Christian and Native American prophecies. There was a day, not long ago, when such a quest would have been an unthinkable subject for me. But now, it seemed that I could not rest until I was fully illumined about these prophecies. It was like a hunger now - like a deep aching need.

CHAPTER XVI

THE LATE AFTERNOON SUN FOUND THE TOLTEC statue sailing down Oak Creek Canyon south of Flagstaff heading for Sedona. I say sailing because that's what it was doing - literally. We were on a narrow, winding road that was dropping 1,000 feet in altitude every four or five miles. I had lost almost all of my braking power as fire and smoke could be detected coming from the brake pads of the truck. There was nowhere to pull over during the rapid descent, thus I lapsed into feverish prayer while carefully sparing what brakes were left. Not until we pulled safely into a rest area near the bottom did I notice the astounding beauty of the canyon. Jessie had panicked all the way down wanting to jump out of the truck and was still recovering from the potential terror of losing control while I checked all the brake pads. They had burned red hot but were not beyond use.

Oak Creek Canyon is an incredible place. The sheer beauty of canyon pine, the massive cliffs of orange and red rock and the crystal clear stream brought tears to my eyes. As I knelt down near a calm eddy in the stream to wash my face, I felt tremendous magic and power in the canyon. This surely was a sacred place. I said a prayer of thanks to the higher forces for the safe passage down the mountainside and for the opportunity to feel the power and energy of such a natural monument. Sedona, for the most part, turned out to be a new-age tinsel town. The three days we spent there, though, were not without real spiritual awakening for me. I learned much about the area and about the Native American reverence for the special landscape and sacred canyons all around us. Here and there, I met people who took their spirituality and emotional healing seriously. But mostly I saw capitalism working overtime in the names of crystal power and Mastercharge. Strangely enough, I had run into Allen, one of the fellows I had met on the first visit to Hopi land. I quickly realized that he was somewhat caught up in *spiritual* profit schemes as there were many people involved with such schemes in that town. Despite all the tinsel though, Sedona is a very magical place. I had never experienced any place like Sedona before, nor have I since. I had an intuitive feeling that the Sedona area would become more and more of a sacred healing place for human beings as time went on and after all the die-hard habits of greed and selfishness began to fade. Many of the local Southwestern Native Americans had come to this area for their most sacred prayers and healing ceremonies. People who were now coming to abuse the special power in the magical canyon realms around Sedona would pay a heavy price. This was the prophecy. It is not a good thing to mislead people with spiritual ideas or to pretend to be a Shaman healer. People who were doing such things were only creating more spiritual karma for themselves. It's not a great thing to make a profit off of spiritual objects like crystals and herbs. It's a much worse thing to make a profit off of spiritual delusion.

I could not bring myself to sell the Toltec totem in Sedona but I'll never forget the last night that I spent there. Soon after a late night swim in the motel pool, I had drifted off to sleep and right into a very realistic and powerful dream. Ever since my drowning, swimming in warm water would always open me up to transcendental realms of experience, especially late at night. But this night brought me one of the most beautiful unconscious experiences that I've ever dreamed for I visited a world that waits for the spiritual awakening of humanity... I visited the planet Venus.

Now I had dreamed and left my body before. I had died and left my body before. I had fasted for many weeks to the brink of physical existence and left my body. But never had I dreamed so real and true as I did the last night in Sedona. Surely, to write about this dream now might evoke some severe skepticism in potential readers for even I can hardly fathom its mystical actuality... though I must go on and tell about my visit to Venus.

Astronomers and scientists tell us that Venus is super hot with tremendous volcanic activity. This is true but true only to our physical senses. There are realms of being all around us here on the planet Earth that we are not able to sense. It is the same on Venus. Physicists have discovered the world of "anti-matter"- a place where time and space cease to exist. This is where we go when we dream and this is where I went after the late night swim.

The first thing I remember is that I was floating gently down through deep and soft clouds of emerald green and golden yellow. The atmosphere around me was rich with nitrates or some other chemical element that stimulates the desire among living beings to thrive and prosper. I could see the sun blazing through the rich haze but never could I have been blinded by directly gazing towards the center of the light. The sun was as large as half the sky but softened by the unbroken cloud cover. When I came to rest on the ground, I immediately noticed that my body was somewhat transparent but still as I remembered in form. I was so tired. I tried to stay awake to enjoy this newfound beauty around me but could not. After a while of quiet resting, I felt someone touch my head. I awoke suddenly to see a radiant, bearded man with caring eyes and gentle hands beckoning me to follow him down towards a distant valley.

Everywhere... on every horizon... around every

plant, tree and rock there was an iridescent golden glow. After a very short walk, I found that we were very near a mountain valley that, at first, seemed to be a hundred miles away. I noticed, too, that the experience of walking was strangely effortless.

"Jonathon, you do remember the day on the beach... you do remember the warm and healing light? We came to baptize you that day and heal your weary soul."

As he was speaking in terms of "we", I wondered who else he was referring to. His eyes sensed my wonder and directed me to my right. There beside me was a very spiritually vivid being. Streams of red and lavender feather-like lights flowed continuously around this person who seemed to very much represent a Native American from the plains of North America.

"Do not be surprised, Jonathon. This is your spirit form."

I looked down to affirm my transparent but still recognizable body and found only the appearance of the spirit that had just stood on my right moments before. I could see an aged, dark body through the streams of red and now violet lights. But yet, to my right stood another radiant being in the form of a woman. She was so extremely beautiful, so pure in heart, that I immediately fell to the ground unable to stand in her presence or to look at her brilliant and perfect soul. Just then, I felt a wave of love and light wash through me in a cleansing and accepting rush.

"Rise up now, Jonathon, and come with us. This is my sister. She is mother and guardian to all the world that you see before you. She has all the blessings from the Grandfather-Grandmother Creator to take care of this world and has already begun to receive many of my children. Look, Jonathon, do you see? Do you see those souls over there?"

I looked in the direction that he was motioning to and, of all things, saw tipi-like structures in a field of goldenrod. Beyond the tipis, in the distance, I could even see herds of buffalo. Then my eyes seemed to become more like visionary screens and I saw many people living in peace and harmony in every direction. I saw elephants with long ivory tusks grazing without fear of poachers. I saw lions, eagles and could hear the songs of dolphins and whales coming from some realm below me. I saw African and Amazonian people dancing around new-born children that were nursing women with milk-laden breasts. People of every race, color and walk of life were living in total peace and in harmony with the world around them. Their food was some kind of mystical fruit as they never had to kill any living thing for nourish-ment. This world appeared to be a place of rest, healing and preparation for further spiritual growth in other more distant worlds.

A river of water was now rushing down my ankles as my heart had begun to weep so hard and long that I feared I was going to wash myself away from this beautiful place. But, instead, a magical garden of plants and flowers grew up where the river had flowed away from me. There, in the middle of the garden, stood the eternal mother of Venus. She was calling for me to come rest again... this time in the *garden* of my tears. Just before I went to sleep, the radiant man who had first welcomed me brought me a piece of the special fruit. I thanked him and will always remember who he was by the scars in the palms of his hands. As I slept in the healing vibrations of the Goddess-Venus, all of my fears and insecurities about the future of humanity were dissolved away. I dreamed of other worlds while lying there in the garden for there are many other realms of spiritual being within our galaxy and beyond waiting for the arrival of human souls.

That night in Sedona, after waking up in the motel room, I needed two or three hours of recovery time before I could realize where I was and what I was doing there. The dream had affected me deeply. I think that my *other self* or soul very nearly left my body for good that night. I surely did not want to leave that world. It seemed as though I had dreamed within a dream and remembered it all. How would I ever relate to others the promise of our afterlife on Venus with Christ and the Mother Goddess without being considered crazy or off the wall? All throughout my life I had experienced vivid dreams often warning me of the need for personal growth and change. I had always followed them, despite the demands made on me by my family and society. And besides, I had probably already experienced the wrath of skeptics and faithless people many times throughout the ages. There was one time, in particular, that came to mind quite clearly. It happened in the late summer of 1977 right after I came out of the forest and ended my three-month fast. My father and stepmother thought that I, being barefoot and penniless, had gone over the deep end. I tried to tell them about my mystical experiences but they did not want to hear about them. Instead, they were convinced that my peaceful and happy state of mind had to be the result of drugs or some mental madness. Before my fast, I had given away all my material things to needy people and what money I had to my sister who was really struggling to take care of her little girl. I was not worried about the future. Having died and come back already once, what did I have to fear? I could go back to work after my fast and quickly earn what things I needed and a place to live. I needed to follow my heart and inner calling first and foremost and that's exactly what I did.

The day I came back to town at the end of my inner quest, I was hungry - very hungry. I went directly to the

Bear's Den at the University of Maine to get something to eat. I grabbed a cheese sandwich at the walk-through deli counter and went in the dining area to eat it. I had evidently neglected to pay for it at the register for, before I had finished eating, a University policeman showed up to escort me out of the station. I admit that my appearance was a little ragged but I would have paid for the sandwich somehow. Well, this little incident proved to be my father's ticket to have me put under "observation" for a while at a local mental hospital. The police had given me a summons. While I showered and cleaned up at my father's house, he found the summons in my pocket. He called the District Court judge and made a deal to put me in for ten days to be sure I was sane.

This began one of the strangest and most painful dramas of my present life. I was checked into the substance abuse and counseling ward even though I was, by now, coming back fully to the material reality. Once inside the center, the doors were locked behind me and I quickly realized that my peace of mind was in grave danger. On the second day I was there, I witnessed the forced drugging of a very gentle and peace-loving soul who had no mental or emotional problems other than a need for some rest. His name was Luke Jordan. Being a lobsterman from a coastal Maine town, he was an honest and hardworking man. He had recently purchased his own boat and was very happy with his life. One day, while pulling traps, he was approached by a boat carrying state drug agents. They were looking for any leads they could find about night drug runs into the many hidden coves in the jagged coastline. Luke had not been involved in any of this type of activity because he was personally against drugs. But one of the agents had slipped a hit of acid into his Pepsi in hopes of retrieving information from him while he hallucinated. Luke had no information for them and had gone into complete mental and physical panic. His wife rushed him to the same observation center that I was at for help.

By the time we met, he was coming down fine and both of us really began to stick together and watch what was really going on in the center around us. We witnessed nurses and counselors use drugs to control and manipulate people towards late night or locked room sexual encounters. I was approached on the second day by a female counselor behind locked doors. The perpetrator would arrange a private counseling session with you and take you to a private room. If you refused the advances, you were recommended for intensive drug therapy. I'll never forget the abuse of one young girl. She was being drugged by her counselor so bad that she could hardly verbalize any words at all. She had come for healing as she had been terribly abused by her father sexually. Now her counselor-psychologist was doing the same. He actually had a routine of drugging and molesting her.

Well, Luke and I wanted no part of this place but we still had eight days to go. The center stood firm to the ten-day observation period once you were in for they were funded by the state according to how many beds were filled. It had been a particularly slow month and we were welcome subjects. By the second night, both Luke and I were afraid to sleep for fear of being drugged so we sat up all night in one of the lounge rooms. I was afraid to eat the food they provided also for the same reason and going without *meat and potatoes* was no problem for me.

On the third morning, Luke asked to call his wife. When he was refused, he got a little upset and raised his voice. Suddenly an alarm went off and four or five people came running down the hall towards him. They pushed him to the floor, pulled down his pants and gave him a shot in the buttocks. Then they locked him into a cell-type room near the nurse station. I was horrified and more determined than ever to stay clear of the same treatment. I figured out a safe time to nap in the day and continued to stay awake at night against the orders of the center director. Two days went by before Luke came to. When he did, I could hear him pleading with mumbled words to be let out. His family had been notified that he had a nervous breakdown and would be in for a long stay.

Just coming out of a three month fast, I was able to perceive the political and financial reality of Luke's forced drugging. The state drug enforcement agency wanted him to have a full nervous breakdown to discredit the true story and cover up their mistake. The center needed more patients at the time to insure financial quotas... thus, I became the next victim. I had gone to the nurse in charge and calmly asked her to let Luke out as, by now, I could detect real panic and pain in his calls for help. The next thing that I remember is the alarm going off and people holding me down on the floor. Luke came out and I went in.

I was drugged extensively for three or four weeks but never was I alone. I had strong spiritual protection and guidance throughout the whole ordeal and was, literally, rescued by a man named Dr. Salveston. He was a psychologist working part-time at the hospital. When we met and talked, he immediately realized what had happened to me and quickly arranged my safe departure from the center and for a safe and controlled withdrawal from the powerful drugs they had forced me to take. He then helped me get established back in the carpentry trade by giving me some remodeling work at his home. I went back to the University of Maine and continued my philosophical and theological studies. Luke had not been so lucky. He was kept under heavy sedation for over a year until his spirit was broken. In all, it took over five years for him to heal from the chemical damage done to his nervous system. Since the whole ordeal, I have never been able to tell this story before now. I know that my Venus dream and my experience of the Goddess in the "garden of my tears" was the real turning point for all my unhealed emotional wounds - both in this life and in past lives.

CHAPTER XVII

ON A DIRECT ROUTE THROUGH THE SOUTH-WEST desert to Albuquerque and points north, the Toltec statue streamed along at 65 or 70 miles an hour towards our home destinations. Jessie was heading for Taos and into a new life of independence and spiritual growth which was what she so desperately needed. I was heading for Santa Fe and towards a profound period of creative and visionary experience. I needed to go inward as I had done before to find purpose and direction in my life. I needed some time alone to question and digest all of the experience of the past winter. The "eclipse" was two months away but yet I felt a major change developing within my unconscious being. It was if some part of my unused mind was being awakened and slowly activated and it was a very emotional time for me. So many unresolved feelings and emotions were surfacing in my soul since the powerful dream in Sedona. It had caused me to remember Luke Jordan and our short sojourn together at the "observation center". That had been a very difficult time for sure but the painful experience was not without great measures spiritual wisdom. I got a first hand look at the "psychological" and "counseling" industry typical of a spiritually bankrupt American society.

This country was not built on a solid spiritual foundation in the first place and what support stones of morality, unity, dignity and equality there were, started crumbling decades ago. I had always loved this country though, despite even my own personal hardships and exposure to political realities. I always thought that somehow Americans would pull together and salvage what is left of this magnificent land. I always thought that Americans would recognize the need to give back to the Native cultures their full dignity and learn from Native American spiritual philosophy... especially since institutionalized Christianity was failing them. But I was coming to realize that it was going to take some kind of Divine intervention and major Earth changes to bring Americans around to higher realities. I was born a dreamer. All my life I had experienced mystical dreams and creative visions which have steadily intensified since the afterlife experience. During the long summer fast of '77, I had many visions about the future of America and about the spiritual future of humanity. As I grew through my thirties, I have stood by and watched many of these visions become reality and it's a painful thing to watch. Most of the time I have just blocked it out. I have needed times of solitude to realign my purpose for fear of losing my intuitive insight. That is all that I did during the summer of 1977. I had not harmed or been a threat to anyone. I connected so deeply with the currents of universal love during those months and saw so much within, that it would take volumes of books to write it down. I was so inspired on creative levels that, even to this day, I drive myself half mad all of the time trying to release it all through music, art and sculpting.

Was I a crazy person because I had no fear of giving all my possessions away and standing alone in the wilderness to face the Eternal Creator? My father sure thought I was crazy. For the life of him, he could not understand my loving trust in the higher forces. He could not understand my compassion and love for people in need. I guess it all went back to my childhood. I remembered many times when my mother would abuse me emotionally and sometimes physically, but I would always end up doing something to please her and make her life easier. I remembered the times I would have to ride two miles to the grocery store on my bike, making three or four trips to get groceries for a week or two because we did not have a car. I would come home sometimes at midnight after folding boxes in a doughnut shop for a half a cent a box trying to earn milk and bread for the next day, and get a very warm feeling when I found my brothers and sister safe and sound in their beds. That was all that mattered to me in those days... that they were safe and sound in their beds. I tried like hell to keep my family together and to understand why my mother had become so abusive, but eventually it all overwhelmed me. I would never change one thing about my childhood if I had the chance. I learned to care about other people and to make sacrifices to ensure the well-being of the ones I loved. Maybe I was born under a benevolent star or something, for I always had strong inner guidance and protection. I was always able to regenerate quickly on emotional levels and move forward.

The drive east through the deserts was long and hot. I spent a lot of time looking back over my own life and over my slow but steady spiritual awakening. I remembered back to the age of thirteen when my mother first took me to a Catholic Church. Being a very shy and spiritually sensitive young man, and never having had any previous religious induction, the experience of the Catholic Church for the first time was one I'll never forget: the strong smells of incense and burning candles gave me eerie sensations of ancient rituals. High above the altar in front of me hung a twenty-foot wooden cross. Affixed to the cross was a bigger than life man who obviously had been tortured badly and nailed up. Simulated streams of red blood poured from his wounds. I was horrified. "What is this place my mother brought me to?" I wondered. "Was this some kind of cult? My

God!... they talk about eating a tortured man's body and drinking his blood." And there was all this talk about the need to confess my sins. What had I done that was so wrong anyway? For years up to that point, every day of my life had been a constant struggle just to keep harmony in the family. There was something terribly wrong with that whole conception of Divinity as far as I was concerned and I learned absolutely nothing about love and the real message of Christ there at that Church.

I think that, somehow, I connected with the real message of Christ even before I was exposed to his teachings in the New Testament while in college. Most all children are born with the love that Christ exemplified and are born very open to the Divine realms. It is the society into which they are born that directs them away from these realms. It is not natural for human beings to repress the intuitive and spiritual side of being. Early Christianity incorporated the mystical aspects of being, but quickly began to condemn and outlaw these aspects of being for they undermined the growing religious-political institution. Religious-political societies have no need for spiritually *enlightened* leaders that teach the real path to truth which exists within the heart of every human being.

I remember feeling spiritually and creatively repressed as a child and, by the age of fifteen, I was terribly angry and hurt for the misguidance. I could have easily gone a very self-destructive route for sure if not for that one stormy day on a San Diego beach. I truly believe that my body and soul were baptized in spirit that day. As each year has passed since, I have learned to follow my heart more and more and I have learned to value spiritual growth and development as first and foremost to any other thing in this life. When we die, we take nothing with us but our own soul. In the end, there is nothing but truth. That is why it is so important to be true to ourselves now while we are here on Earth.

It was only natural for me to follow the mystical path. After all, nothing in this material life would ever be as real to me as the experience of the afterlife. There was something eternal and supreme about the afterlife that, for me anyway, will never be matched by any mortal experience. Human beings need and desire to know this realm. Today, more than ever, people are yearning for spiritual guidance. They are yearning to let go of religious and political delusions and they are yearning to go back to more natural, Earth-connected experiences. My whole life has been characterized by this very yearning. I always had felt a natural connection to the Earth. My grandfather once brought me a pair of moccasins from an Arizona Reservation. I was about thirteen years old then and my mother used to actually threaten to beat me if I wore them anywhere in public. I used to throw them out my back window before I left for school and then change into them. I loved those moccasins. By the time I finally let go of them, there was nothing at all left of the soles. Looking back, I suddenly realized that a strange connection between my past and future had manifested profoundly through the experience of these moccasins. After all these years, my feet had carried me back to Arizona and the Native American Reservations. My life had always been so spiritually directed and orientated, even as a child. I just never realized it until I started developing spiritually. It is the same for any human being. We are all born from spirit, live in spirit and return to spirit. Anyone can become self-aware of the spiritual forces that are constantly at work all around us and within us trying to guide us towards the Divine.

We all have issues to work out in this life. We all have to learn to be honest with ourselves. We are never alone. The great life force of Eternal Creation penetrates every human being to the core. Native Americans recognized and honored the universal life force in everything. They were truly on the right path to Divinity. What right did anyone have to condemn or destroy their cultures? What right does anyone have to condemn or criticize things they don't understand? Despite all the condemnation and destruction of Native cultures, the seeds of spirituality can never be destroyed. The evidence of this can be seen in the growing emergence of Native American philosophy everywhere in American society. Many of the great Native American leaders spoke about the inevitable return to their spiritual beliefs by people of all race, color and creed. The same return to a more natural and love-centered society is foretold in the last chapter of the New Testament. It is written that the return of Christ will usher in a new age and that there will be one thousand years of peace and deathless healing for all the spiritually awakened souls. The transition would not be an easy one, I thought, for the jaws of hate, destruction and violence sure had a strong hold on the collective soul of humanity these days. Peace seemed to be more and more an elusive experience in this world.

After dropping Jessie off in Taos, I went directly to Santa Fe. It did not take me long to settle in and get creative. Every sunrise seemed to bring me new realizations and spiritual awakening. I started writing spiritual folk songs and developing rapidly with my music. I began painting the most profound and delicate paintings of my life thus far. Never had I been exposed to so much artwork in one area. There were galleries upon galleries in Santa Fe and, soon, my sculptures were taken on commission by one of them.

I missed my children terribly. I had never been apart from them for more than a few days. It had been six weeks since they departed and I felt that I desperately needed to fly back to Maine for a visit with them. I would have to wait though. The eclipse was coming in July and I needed to be ready physically and emotionally to receive the *winged messenger* that would surely bring me new vision and direction in my life. All of the deep levels of anguish and pain that I was feeling from being apart from my children was a part of my purification for now: I had to let go of everything and become detached from the emotional world as much as possible. I had developed into a very passionate and loving human being. I loved life. I loved the experience of close relationships. I could never really live without them ultimately. I just needed to make a small sacrifice and go without a close relationship for now. My sons and I were bonded in the heart. I had to know that they would be all right despite my growing intuition that they were not well taken care of by their mother back in Maine.

CHAPTER XVIII

SOMETHING VERY STRANGE HAPPENED TO ME IN SANTA FE. Within days of my arrival, I began to experience deeper levels of reality and *being* that had previously been unknown to me or only imagined. It was as if all life around me took on a magnetic glow and I could see the intricate connectedness of all things. Plants, trees, rocks, the sky - everything seemed to be radiating mystical light. Day after day, the experience increased causing me to slow down the pace of my life and contemplate more. I realized that the world around me was sacred and alive with spiritual essence. I could see the deeper realities of karma and purpose in people and in all the human relationships around me including my own interactions with others. At times, the magnitude of the intuitive vision would increase allowing me to see the realities of past life experience in others.

I could not control or direct this intuitive vision. It would just open up at the most unusual times and in the most unusual places like the check-out line in a grocery store. Auric shades of purple, lavender, green, blue and yellow would surround the forms of most everything creating a living kaleidoscope. There were people, though, that had no glow whatsoever. I wondered about this and came to realize that these people were spiritually closed off. There were people, too, that had very weak but distinguishable glows which revealed neglected spirituality. The strangest thing about it all was the fact that I could always see the spiritual light in natural objects like rocks. Why couldn't I see the same in every human being? We are all material in body. This concerned me but I was in no condition to analyze or rationalize these things during the intuitive states. I just flowed along with the experience and, as each day passed, I became more and more an open receiver to the spiritual realms. The eclipse was coming soon and I was being prepared for powerful revelations about my future purpose and about the spiritual condition of humanity. Two years before learning anything about the July eclipse and the Hopi prophecies, I had carved the image of the moon passing directly over the sun on the prophecy totem. Four or five years earlier than that, I had dreamed about it. There was a greater purpose to my journey west - greater than the experience with the Hopi people and their prophecies.

During my stay in Santa Fe, I learned so much about how people are spiritually interrelated with each other and with the world around them. The life force which flows with ever changing currents of Earth elements, water and air through all living things has no boundaries. It has no beginning and no end. Every part of our being is connected to every other being. This is why our thoughts and feelings are so important. Because there is no separation in our bodies and minds from the electro-magnetic matrix of elements, our thoughts actually do affect the world around us. Human beings exist within a sort of electro-magnetic soup. Many Native cultures were sensitive to this aspect of being. Western culture, which placed reason over intuition, has been, for the most part, blind to this.

Our minds are powerful receivers and transmitters, both passive and active. During the passive states, we attract objects and other people according to the thoughts that we harbor, as all our thoughts have a certain electro-magnetic spectrum. The nature of faith is definitely related to the positive levels of the passive state. If our desire and need for something is true, committed and intense enough, whether this something be relatively good or bad, we will, eventually, manifest it into our life. The same goes for the negative aspects of the passive state. Fear, doubt and confusion are the rulers of this realm and a person will attract experiences and people that reflect whatever is going on in their minds. Faith in things not yet seen, touched, held or known is what moves humanity forward and is seen as the grace of our Creator. Lack of faith is negative simply because of what our minds will randomly attract to fill voids and pockets of indecision. In other words, a person who knows what they want and has begun to cast a steady focus will attract what they need to fulfill the form that they envisioned. Each thought that we have has a certain electro-magnetic quality, just as each object and each soul has a certain electro-magnetic quality. Faith is a great power. Human beings will one day rediscover the power of faith. As the world falls deeper and deeper into the political and economic chaos, faith in Christ, faith in our Creator and faith in the spiritual realities of our existence will increase among many, many people. Not until then will we really understand the positive aspects of the passive states of being. Too many people focus on material things and selfish gain. Thus, great imbalances are created in the world because of it.

The same principle of electro-magnetics applies to our active states. We can actually project our thoughts-our visions into the material world. When we project our mental energy, we cause change. Herein lies the real essence of human experience. Since the earliest ages, human beings have had to deal with the changes in the world around them caused directly by the thoughts that they project. Every time a person projects a negative, destructive or angry thought, they set in motion a particular energy release in the collective mainstream of human consciousness that, eventually, ripples back to its source. A good example of this is the increasing wave of violence that is sweeping the planet today. Destructive thoughts are running rampant.

Positive thoughts, on the other hand, are not without great measure today. Many people are coming alive spiritually and learning to project love and healing energy. This type of energy is the most powerful... thanks to the Goddess. The power of love and spiritual faith is the only force holding the balance in terms of human experience. If it were not for this power, the world would surely collapse into utter chaos. It is the children that, for the large part, keep humanity balanced. Young children are fountains of love and healing energy. During the mystical and visionary experiences while in Santa Fe, I was able to see streams of positive energy coming from the hearts of children. Most all souls are born in the faithful, passive state of being and are open to the currents of universal love and creation. Until a child is conditioned to think and project thoughts according to social conventions, the currents of love received by the passive mind are magnified by the active mind and projected outward to their parents and the whole electro-magnetic matrix surrounding them. One of the most important teachings of Christ is this exact realization. We must become as children to enter the kingdom of heaven. We must be spiritually born again to the pure states of consciousness of early childhood. This does not mean abandoning our adult responsibilities. It simply means that we need project more purely good and love-centered thoughts. Unless conditioned to do so through fear, anger or whatever, a very young child will never project a negative thought as a natural response to any association in life. This is the great miracle of human creation and re-creation. Have you ever noticed that some elderly people that have found happiness and love in their lives will naturally return to the *child* consciousness before they pass over?

Native Americans were, for the most part, well aware of this miracle of human re-creation. Thoughts of love and celebration were consciously and purposely radiated out into the world every day through prayer offerings of thanks, beautiful ceremonies and daily activities rich and alive with spiritual meaning. They worked continuously to keep a *childlike* openness to the Divine aspects of being. It was their custom to leave their young children with the elderly because the child-like love and understanding of the elders could communicate great wisdom to the children - something lost in our modern society!

A faithful passive mind combined with a love-centered, focused, active mind is the most effective mind of all. Native American cultures fostered just such mental development. Western *man*, though, has largely existed through the active realms of thought, running around the world projecting selfish ideas. The traditional political and religious forces have suppressed the development of the faithful, passive realms of thought which harbor intuition. This has resulted in spiritually weak societies and explains why so many people are turning towards Native American spirituality for direction. People are also reaching out for new conceptions of our Creator. The female - Goddess aspects of existence can no longer be repressed.

What exactly is the faithful passive mind, I wondered? Could it be likened to the eternal promise within the darkness of the cyclic return of the warm, healing and life-giving light? Could it be likened to the very deepest desire and yearning of a person - any person, great or small, that eventually begins to manifest into material reality after a long period of ardent and dedicated faith?

I had a dream one night in Santa Fe while sleeping on the couch in my temporary studio. I dreamt that I was in a terrible prison somewhere in an area of tropical jungle. I struggled through what seemed to be all night to get out of that prison. Finally, after fighting off guards, mad dogs and after climbing over many barbed-wire fences, I was able to escape into the jungle. I ran for miles and miles until I came to an old stone house. There were two people inside: a tall fair-skinned woman and a shy, young boy. I had the feeling that the boy was me, or the child in me and the woman was my spiritual mother. The house was full of strong aromas of drying herbs and flower perfumes. The woman was so healthy and natur-ally beautiful as her every thought and action was in harmony with nature and the universe. She had long before spiritually blossomed but was forced to flee into a remote and solitary life. Somehow, I was aware that her spirituality had been a threat to the patriarchal leaders of her culture.

After a while of partaking in fresh tropical fruit, nuts, herbal tea and her healing presence, she led me out of the house to an old and grown-over stone road. Soon, we were standing on the edge of a massive gorge. I could hear the thunderous roar of water coming from the depths of the gorge as she led me to the steps of an ancient pyramid. Carefully, we climbed the steep steps one by one stepping over vines, branches and patches of tropical moss. Upon reaching the top, we came to the temple entrance. It was at this point that I awoke. It was July 11, 1991. I had been fasting for three days preparing for the eclipse. Like so many times before, my unconscious mind had interrelated with my conscious mind through the dream state. Today, I would enter the temple.

For two or three weeks prior to the eclipse, the *Goddess* began appearing to me. There was no doubt that my emotional and physical bodies were being cleansed with healing light and unconditional love. Now, I suppose, many people would think that I had gone off the deep end. But, really, I hadn't. I had just become so open and so aware of life's beauty that I was able to experience the Divine Creator directly through the souls of two or three women that crossed my path at the time. They were my guides to a very special experience of natural beauty and mystical union with the sacred life energy of Santa Fe's surrounding mountains. I was first taken to Cochiti Falls north of the city and near Native American territory. There, I bathed in the melting snows of pristine mountain ravines where lions and golden eagles still live in ancient domains. The friend who had brought me was my female double. She was born on the same day in May as I and, although she was much younger in terms of measured time, her soul was the same age as mine. For a few days we gave each other companionship and unconditioned love never wanting to spoil the intuitive experience of the God and the Goddess within each other through emotional and sexual intercourse. We just were happy to touch the sky together.

I was then led into the high mountain valleys and aspen-lined canyon streams directly above Santa Fe. For a couple of days, I experienced one of the most beautiful places on Earth. There are no words for those mountains. They stand like islands of paradise in the middle of volcanic laced desert plains. In early July, the high meadows come alive with flowers of extreme and delicate magic. Patches of ice and snow linger on the north slopes gently feeding warming ponds with cool, oxygen laden waters. I was with the Goddess again. We lay silent and peacefully together next to these ponds and in the face of eternal creation totally free and clothed only in wildflowers and forest incense. Have you ever hugged a tree naked? Every moment with her in those mountains was beyond physical orgasms. I was one with nature's passion and procreative force. I'll never forget those days. I still carry dried mushrooms and herbs from those mountains and from those couple of days with the Goddess in my medicine bag. I ration them out very lovingly and carefully to special friends and to myself in times of spiritual need.

It was after these experiences of the Goddess, after many weeks of mystical *seeing*, after three days of fasting, and after many years of dedication to spiritual visions and direction that I was ready to enter the temple.

I come to you, now, Grandmother Creator...
*   in truth and in Love*

I ask only for light in my path
through the shadows and illusions
*   of my undeveloped self.*

Please guide me here..........
Please allow the beauty and purpose
of this soul to be understood.

In the name of Jesus,
*   and all the great lights*
*   of human kind................*

*   Amen*

CHAPTER XIX

A S I STUMBLED HUNGRY AND EXHAUSTED down the steep mountainside back towards my studio on the outskirts of Santa Fe, I knew that it would take me months and even years to fully understand the meaning of the visionary experience that I had just gone through. I was sunburned, desperately thirsty and emotionally drained for I had spent most of the day sitting high in the mountains in quiet solitude while focusing my inner eye towards the Southern latitudes of Central Mexico and the eclipse. Shortly after climbing up the mountainside and after clearing my mind of all mundane concerns, I had drifted right back to the dream state of the night before and back to the steps of the pyramid temple.

The first moments after entering the temple were beautiful. The woman who had led me there, step by step over the jungle paths and up the steep pyramid side, had now exposed her inner light which bathed my soul in waves of universal understanding. I had never felt such intense healing energy as her aura glowed like an iridescent amethyst. She then led me down a long, incredible passageway that was about twelve feet in width and the same in height. There were no golden statues or ivory mosaics. Instead, there were paintings on every wall and ceiling rich and alive with fresh tones, scarlet reds, bright yellows and hazy whites. The paintings depicted scenes from all realms of plant, animal and human existence and they portrayed the sacred, divine nature of each realm. Every scene was magically interconnected with all the other scenes creating a mural that seemed to flow along the walls as if alive. It seemed that the artists and designers who created the murals came from a culture that did not look to some transcendental God, Goddess or Divinity to find heaven and universal harmony. They lived as Gods and Goddesses and were aware of the divine and sacred nature of all human activity on the face of this planet, including the painful and tragic times. Life was depicted as a beautiful tapestry that was still in the making. It was then, after this creative realization, that I sensed levels of sadness rise up from the depths of my being and I understood that many human beings in the present world were not the least bit aware of their own divinity. They were not aware of how sacred every breath of air, every return of spring and every gift of passion really was. Perhaps ultimate happiness was not in some *state of mind* or in some fantasy of *pearly gates* and patriarchal domination of the human soul. Perhaps happiness was in the art of living - the realms of human activity that cause spiritual growth and development while in the material forms. Even the realms of sexual experience in the paintings of the temple walls portrayed beautiful visions and cosmic illumination above the bodies of men and women who were joined together in physical union. The Creator did not give human beings divine senses so that we could feel guilty about them. If honored and kept sacred, these senses could be experienced as doorways to peace and extreme contentment while in the material world.

The sadness that I had felt in the corridors of living tapestry quickly dissolved away as we entered the center of the temple. Steady heartbeat rhythms were now surrounding my being and my soul was immediately taken up into a journey of vibrational revelations. The pyramid chamber was afloat now and we were moving through different levels of existence like the beam of a light ray moving through the passages of time. I could see the eclipse beginning and the blazing light of the sun was intensifying on the outer edges of the shadow disk. It was as if a great cycle of time was ending and another was going to begin. My vision of the eclipse extended both into the past and future and could see other, larger cycles of eclipses of which the event, now in front of me, was a part. I was drawn to peer within the shadows of the disk and it was then and there that I watched the drama of human tribulation unfold.

"Oh God"... I thought, "no".

I suddenly remembered that there was a sleeping prophet that once spoke about some strange events that would befall humanity near the year two thousand. This sleeping prophet was Edgar Cayce. Most of his mystical and intuitive abilities were devoted to helping people heal from physical and spiritual ailments but there were times when he would see directly into the future of mankind. During many of his psychic trances, he would often relay the same message back to be recorded: "In the last years of the twentieth century, there will be large scale crustal displacements caused by human beings." I had never understood Cayce's predictions before the temple revelations but, during the eclipse, I had watched the immediate future of Earth and the collective soul of humanity unfold in vivid color. The things that I saw were never related to any particular date or time. They were related to human consciousness and human activity on the surface of the globe. It was a horrendous sight at first as I watched the whole planet become unstable within the gravitational and magnetic fields of its shifting axis. Major volcanic activity erupted on the floor of the Atlantic Ocean which set in motion massive movements in the continental plates. Giant walls of water wiped out whole cities as the world's oceans' levels also became subject to sudden crustal displacement. The years preceding this upheaval had seen a sharp increase in earthquakes and drastic changes in weather patterns which caused devastating floods in the northern hemisphere and droughts in the southern hemisphere.

All of these changes were directly related to human activity and consciousness. Human beings had altered the balance of surface mass on the planet and had failed to live in harmony with the Earth's ecosystem. The visionary experience that I had during the eclipse was unlike anything that I had ever known before. I seemed to be intellectually and spiritually aware during the whole vision. I was able to see through the mask of material change and through seemingly chaotic events of the near future. On some deep inner level, I knew why the Earth was changing and why humanity had come to the brink of total destruction once again. The most important real-ization of all that came to me in the temple and which still burns in my conscious mind with a fever to be communicated to as many souls as possible is this: At an ever increasing pace, human beings are destroying the balance of the Earth by pumping oil out of the crustal mass. Crude oil is very heavy. One barrel of crude oil weighs about 500 pounds. Human beings are burning up millions of barrels every day which transfers into billions and trillions of pounds. So much of the Earth's crustal mass is up in the sky now that every day of planetary stability that goes by is a miracle.

Many, many thousands of years ago, the Earth went through a dramatic change. It was a time when, for whatever reasons, the planet shifted its axis to find a new balance with the gravitational and magnetic forces of the solar system. The exact angle of the axis, along with the rotational speed of the planet were determined by the mass of Earth's crustal layers. There is geological and biological evidence all over the surface of this planet that many of these shifts have occurred and have coincided with major evolutionary turning points in the tree of life and in this solar system. If it were not for a major catastrophic change of the surface of this planet by which the dinosaurs and their lush forests were destroyed, humanity would not have oil at all. Oil is actually the remains of living mass which was concentrated and buried in once low places. Dinosaurs were incredible fertilizing machines. They helped create tremendous masses of plant life which eventually turned to peat. It takes 100 feet of plant and animal remains compressed to make one foot of peat. It takes 100 feet of peat compressed and heated to make one level foot of oil. Not only are human beings beginning to disrupt the gravitational balance of the Earth by pumping so much mass from the planet's crust, they are, literally "raising the dead". In the last chapter of the bible, St. John talks about this... "the beast shall rise". Are we not raising all the monsters that once roamed this planet by burning their physical remains into the atmosphere?

During the temple vision, I became aware of the deeper, more spiritual implications of the mass burning of oil. I could see an aura of greed and selfishness surrounding the oil economy which was destroying the spiritual balance of humanity as well. The displacement of mass from the Earth's crust is the reflection in the material world of displacement on a much more profound and important level - the level of balance and harmony in human experience. If human beings were created in the image of their Creator, then it stands to reason that we are creating our future right now. We cannot continue to create a world that is ecologically and economically unbalanced. The Earth cannot hold its present axis stability much longer. Human beings cannot continue to exist on the surface of this planet or anywhere else in the universe if they don't find a spiritual balance and begin to develop towards a true state of equity for all and towards a more love-healing state of being which includes all living things. Thus, I saw the pumping of oil directly related to mankind's past. Humanity, like an individual during a time of emotional or spiritual distress, is trying to hold on to the past. We are resorting to violence and consumption on the level of the monster meat and plant eaters of the distant past. The burning of oil into the atmosphere is very much related to the human condition and to the development of a spiritual consciousness that is free from the *dead* weight of the past.

Yes, during the eclipse, I could see the *beasts* of horror and greed rising up out of the oceans and I could see them eating up the forests, mountains, birds, fish and animals. Some of the machines that humans created to devour the ecosystem even looked like dinosaurs. But the strangest thing of all was the fact that the machines were fueled by the remains of dinosaurs. I could see many drastic imbalances of mass and energy on the surface of the planet. Large scale crustal displacements were everywhere and were not just empty cavities in the ground left by pumping oil. The distribution of material wealth, food and human dignity had displaced the balance in the collective soul of humanity. One thing that all human beings can be sure of is that the basic creative impulse of the universe is towards balance and harmony even if it means destruction and re-alignment. There will be a "new Earth" someday but not before a period of major change. People may tend to think about the possibility of catastrophic change as being terrible and tragic but the reality is that such change will be good for the Earth and for the human soul in the long run.

There were other truths revealed to me during the eclipse about the future of mankind. I remember seeing the great pyramid of Egypt exploding. The whole top section blew up into a million pieces and a whirl of anti-gravity, anti-material force came out of some secret chamber that had been hidden deep within the stone for thousands of years. The force grew and expanded out to every corner of the world and was sucking all the forms of exchange - money - into another dimension. There were people everywhere going crazy because their material systems of security were suddenly gone. It was as if every human being had been cast onto the same level of material experience. I then saw the archangels come down to harvest the children of creation... the ones who had remained in peace and love after all the money was gone and not the ones who had turned to anger and violent means to hold on to old possessive and selfish habits. The purpose of the pyramid energy was clear to me. It was the force of equalization and the power of truth. The strangest thing about the pyramid vision was a realization I experienced about a year or so later after the eclipse. I happened to really notice, for the first time, the pyramid on the back of American dollars. I couldn't believe it! The top of the pyramid is gone and is replaced with the mystical, third eye. That image of the eye is a very ancient symbol and represents the higher conscious ness and a realm where all our acts and deeds, especially our exchanges, are recorded for the eternity of human existence. There is nothing that goes unseen as everything is recorded in the collective unconsciousness. One can hide wrong acts and wrong motives from other people but never from the *eye* of the Creator or the higher realms of knowing. The power of ancient and mystical truth has remained steadfast and true throughout the whole of this material age as the symbols on American money reveal.

All of the future changes and events in the *human drama* that I experienced during the temple vision will most likely come to pass. There have been prophecies about these climactic times for thousands of years. I think that our Creator was aware of the lessons and growth issues of human experience even before he-she actually manifested on Earth. There was likely a clear and well-defined purpose to the development of mankind on the third planet out from the sun, just as there was on Mars in the past and just as there will be on Venus in the future. Children today are being conditioned for great planetary change with all of its aspects whether it be the violent and horrible or the super-natural and beautiful-magical transformations. Just look at the cartoons, movies and video games that program our children's minds, I thought. Everything has a purpose. As the children of today grow into adulthood, the things that they are being conditioned to now will begin to manifest. There will be tremendous violence and horror for sure, but not without its opposite: spiritual magic and beauty.

Yes, human beings today are experiencing the manifestation of prophecy. We will not be alone though. There are divine forces at work on this planet everyday in great measure. During the eclipse, I saw many *angels* or advanced souls walking on Earth guiding and pro-tecting the development of the sacred seed of humanity - the seed of the future that exists in the hearts of people all over this world who yearn for more than selfish, material expansion. The forces of greed and destruction will come to fear these people for sure as they begin to enter the realms of profound spiritual consciousness but it will not matter. The fulfillment of prophecy will come to pass. Venus waits like a silent song and the Goddess has, long ago, forgiven the God.

The temple vision lasted for many hours, it seemed. I saw beautiful things over and above the planetary change and destruction. I saw the collective human soul; the very essence of the Creator, rising up into a new world - a new consciousness of love and humanitarianism. My vision transcended Earth bound experience and I was able to perceive the larger cycles of human development. The collective human soul was not born on Earth. We were only entrusted with this giant garden. We were meant to use and enjoy the garden as long as we protect and preserve it. One of the great lessons of being human is to give back to life what we take and to sustain and nurture the life forms which give us fruit and being. We must do this for our children, our future and for the continual progression of the God-Goddess-Creator towards eternal being, free from the cycles of destruction.

CHAPTER XX

MY LIFE IN SANTA FE AFTER THE ECLIPSE soon became somewhat hollow and unconnected. I missed my sons very much and I missed having a garden. Even as a child, I had always been able to ground my inner mystical nature with the Earth by planting gardens. I could sense that my sons were needing me and that they were not doing well back in Maine with their mother. In late July, I flew to Maine for a week to follow up on my intuition. Sure enough, they were having a hard time with their mother and her abusive, alcoholic boyfriends. They had been neglected and exposed to fits of drunken rage more than once. I spent most of the week with my sons on the Atlantic coast and on the shores of clear, spring-fed lakes. It was a healing time for all three of us for sure. I'll never forget the day we all bathed in the Atlantic Ocean in Acadia National Park. The ocean has a way of cleansing the human soul of emotional pain and hurt. After the week was over, I knew what I had to do. I needed to come home and bring stability back to the lives of my sons. My artistic and mystical dreams would have to wait. As I prepared to fly back to Santa Fe to close up my studio, I talked the situation over with the boys and promised them that I would be back as soon as I possibly could.

By early August, I was back in Santa Fe packing the trailer for the long drive home. I happened to call Francisco to let him know that I was going to be heading east and to see if he needed any help standing the totem. He told me that things had not been good regarding the prophecy totem and that it had set off a lot of political trouble. That night, after talking with Francisco, I laid still in quiet meditation and realized that I had to go get the totem from the Hopi Reservation. I never related well to politics and I certainly did not want to see Francisco struggling with the opposing aspects of his culture more than was naturally destined for him. In my heart I knew what I had to do even though I did not understand the spiritual reality of it all at the time. What would I do with the prophecy totem and how would I transport it all the way back east?

As I drove over to Arizona and the Hopi Mesas, I realized that my political journey was just beginning... not ending. I had a strange feeling that my future in this life was now interwoven with the struggles of Native Americans and the rebirth of their spiritual philosophy. Somehow, the true message of Christ had a direct relationship to Native American spiritual philosophy. My future fate was also interwoven with all people who were becoming more spiritually conscious of the Goddess aspect; the love aspect of universal creation. No great raptures of destruction ever befell humanity from the worship of "Mother Earth". I wished that I could say the same about the worship of a "Transcendent Father", but I could not. The lessons of my journey to Hopi land were clear to me now. Among other truths, I was meant to become aware of and realize the prophecies of many Native Americans about the coming "Earth purification" and the return of the "Great White Brother" or the "Peacemaker" - who is, in all reality, Jesus Christ. The totem, heavy and burdensome at times, had been a sort of cross for myself and Francisco to bear. The heart of the totem cross was formed by the eagle: the great Thunderbird. Francisco saw the hidden reality in it all and so did I. The actual totem, the piece of pine log, really did not matter anymore for the spiritual message of the Thunderbird had been seeded in our hearts and in our souls. Where would I go from this point in my spiritual growth, I wondered, as I drove away from Francisco's house and off of the Hopi Mesas escorted by brand new Hopi Police cars. Perhaps the cross that I was meant to bear was the gift of retribution to the cause of Native American spiritual philosophy. I would come to accept that burden fully in time with faith and hope that my own anglo culture would realize the message of beauty and love that was nearly lost with the attempted destruction of Native American Cultures. The truth is that Christ spent many more years walking and teaching on this continent than in the "Holy Lands" of the Middle East. The sooner all Americans became aware of this, the sooner America would become a real nation of peace and prosperity. Perhaps it was too late. Perhaps the great lusty beast of greed had a strangle hold on the Native American cultures themselves. Sitting Bull said it would happen this way in the end.

I must admit that feelings of despair gripped my soul for days while I slowly made my way north and east towards Maine. The despair that I felt was for the sad spiritual condition of humanity as a whole. So much opportunity for love and peace had been lost and now it seemed that the only hope for humanity lay in the manifestation of both the Christian and Native American spiritual prophecies. My decision to visit South Dakota and the western territory of the Sioux surely did nothing to lighten my feelings of despair. It only made them worse. Here, again, was another beautiful culture forced away from their spiritual ways and forced out of there sacred lands: the Black Hills. Today, the Black Hills are littered with cheap tourist signs as the once sacred places of these mountains are exploited by anglo capitalists. Places like Jewel Cave had become nothing more than holiday side shows. It was here, at places like Jewel Cave, that the Sioux people would come to hear the songs of Mother Earth as the wind rushed in and out of the many secret cave openings on the sides of the mountains. It was here that they would make their special prayers and bury their loved ones as they believed that the spirits of creation inhabited these special mountains. Now they are forbidden from these sacred places and forced to live in the Badlands of Pine Ridge and Rosebud or in the fabricated housing projects of Rapid City. The Black Hills had been stolen from them. There was nothing else to say. There was no excuse. The Sioux never asked for much. Like all of the Native American tribes, they only asked to be left alone in their homelands to practice their own spiritual beliefs. But it was not meant to be. A great sacrifice of culture had to be made on this planet – a sacrifice greater than any before in human history. Sitting Bull, Chief Joseph and other Native American leaders realized this years ago. Humanity, as a whole, is still young and immature. The lessons of love, peace, dignity, honor and respect are hard lessons for some. In the future, human beings may not be so quick to rape and destroy the planet or other cultures. They may learn to live in harmony which seems to be the only way of life that prospers towards eternity. We must learn the lessons here before we ever travel - physically or spiritually - to other places, planets or cultures in the solar system.

Yes, I thought, someday I would return to the Hopi Mesas and to the sacred places of the West but not before telling the story of my spiritual awakening: *The Awakening of Red Feather*. Somewhere within my soul, Red Feather resides. This I know. He (or she) comes and goes but always appears to my intuitive mind to guide and direct me. I have heard that Red Feather appears to others much the same. It's true. There are other writers out there that I've never met who are also being visited and guided by some mystical being named Red Feather. Who is this Red Feather anyway, I wondered? Is this being an old Native Shaman or some ancient god? I don't know. There have been times when I thought Red Feather was some aspect of Christ. There are some people who believe that Christ has manifested in many human forms from all walks of life over the past two thousand years: in effect, never leaving his people. I am inclined to believe that this may be true as Christ loved the children of Earth much too deeply to ever be separated from them for so many, many years. Perhaps Christ lived a life, or many life times as a Native American. Who can say? We know very little about the true reality of the human soul despite all of our technological advances.

In the three years that have passed since I arrived back in Maine and got resettled with my sons, I've come to realize that most people are still very closed-minded to the emerging facts about the relationship between Christ and the Native American traditions. But these people are closed off altogether to the real message of love and humanitarianism that Christ taught. There are people, though, who are, in increasing numbers, coming to realize that the message of Christ was very much the same message of many Native American spiritual teachings. A powerful example can be seen in the passage of the New Testament where Christ goes to the mountains to fast, to face his fears and to find the truth within his heart. This teaching is one of the most important teachings of traditional Native Americans - the *vision quest*. Don't ever be afraid of facing the demons within or being alone in times of emotional desperation. There is a place within every human soul that radiates universal light, love and truth. One of our lessons in being human is to find this altar and to take special care of it. We are meant to realize our true spiritual nature behind the mask of the material world. If we do this, we will automatically take care of Mother Earth and respect all the souls around us.

The most important truths that I have learned from all my conscious and mystical experiences over the past 39 years of my life, I think, can be summed up in the following words: There is a higher purpose and meaning to the seemingly chaotic drama of human existence on the planet Earth. There is a great lesson to be learned from the clashing of institutionalized Christianity and Native American spiritual philosophy. It's a lesson of respect, honor and love for the female aspect of being – whatever level of being you can think of - human, animal or planetary. There is destiny to being... individuals are born into this life with certain dominant and re-occurring themes: lessons of life and love. It is the same on the collective level of cultural history.

Our Creator or God is surely both male and female energy as we are created in our Creator's image as male and female. (The Church Patriarchy likely deleted any and all references to the Goddess from the Bible.) Human beings must realize the mistakes made by dominant patriarchal leaders in many old cultures and rectify them. There is always danger in extremes. In terms of our conceptions of the Creator, humanity needs to find the balance between the God and the Goddess. The reflection of this need is everywhere in modern society. Our Creator is not perfect and the same hierarchy of child-parent-grandparent that is reflected here in the material world of humans likely exists in the universe. Think about it. If our Creator can be understood as an evolving Being which may have made some mistakes, then a lot of rational understanding can be made out of the current human situation.

We are spiritual beings and our souls transcend the material world. This I learned from three direct encounters with the afterlife and the teachings of both Christ and Native American Shamans speak to the spiritual aspect of our beings.

The collective soul of humanity most likely was not born on Earth but was seeded or transported here as the planet cooled into a comfortable and fertile garden. (It was surely part of the Divine plan to have the giant reptiles help fertilize this garden of Earth.) There is evidence mounting up all around modern researchers to support such ideas. The theme of the *garden* in creation stories has a real basis, however, along with the responsibility entrusted to human beings. We are creators of the world now. If we fail to manage this world well, then the human seed will not just vanish. Human beings are the expression of their Creator and our Creator is in this for the long haul. That is the lesson of the prophecies. The planet Venus is a virgin world waiting for the spiritual birth of humanity. ("New Earth" talked about in the Bible.)

There is truth in the prophecies as there is wisdom in the secret places of the heart...

It is June, 1994 and I am ending this story for now. These days, I sometimes see myself as only a spiritual reporter. I have tried my best to convey the message of the prophecies as they came to me over the past ten years or so. Let me tell you that there used to be a day when I really doubted the reality of such a being as Christ, even after drowning and experiencing that higher reality. But I do not have any doubts whatsoever now. There are higher forces at work all over this planet preparing for great Earth changes. This you can be sure of.

Back in the forested hills of Maine, my sons and I have planted larger and larger gardens during the summers these past few years. We grow hundreds and hundreds of pumpkins, an experience which is very good for the children. It gives them a little business in the fall and a strong connection to the Earth. It's strange how life unfolds sometimes. I had a dream in Santa Fe that my studio was full of pumpkin seeds and they all turned into seashells. I'm not quite sure of the spiritual message that dream brought, but it's unfolding in the course of my life.

I have had a few years to rest and regenerate before my next journey; but soon I will have to fulfill a new spiritual responsibility now developing in my life. Perhaps we will meet on this journey. I hope so...

May Christ be with you.

May Red Feather be with you.

ABOUT THE AUTHOR

As a writer, artist, musician, sculptor and astrologer, Jonathon has a deep interest in the present course and future of humanity. His philosophy is very simple and Earth based: learn the lessons of love, life and dignity that we are meant to learn during our journeys here on this blue star and remember that our soul is the only thing that matters in the end. Jonathon spends time in both Maine and Taos, New Mexico working to promote the spiritual philosophy to which he has been awakened. Just look for the "Medicine Bear".

Other books by Jonathon Ray
"The Last Eclipse – Planetary Change and Universal Being"